KEEP OUR WORLD GREEN

Why Humans Need Gardens, Parks and Public Green Spaces

Frieda Wishinsky

Illustrated by
Sara Theuerkauf

ORCA BOOK PUBLISHERS

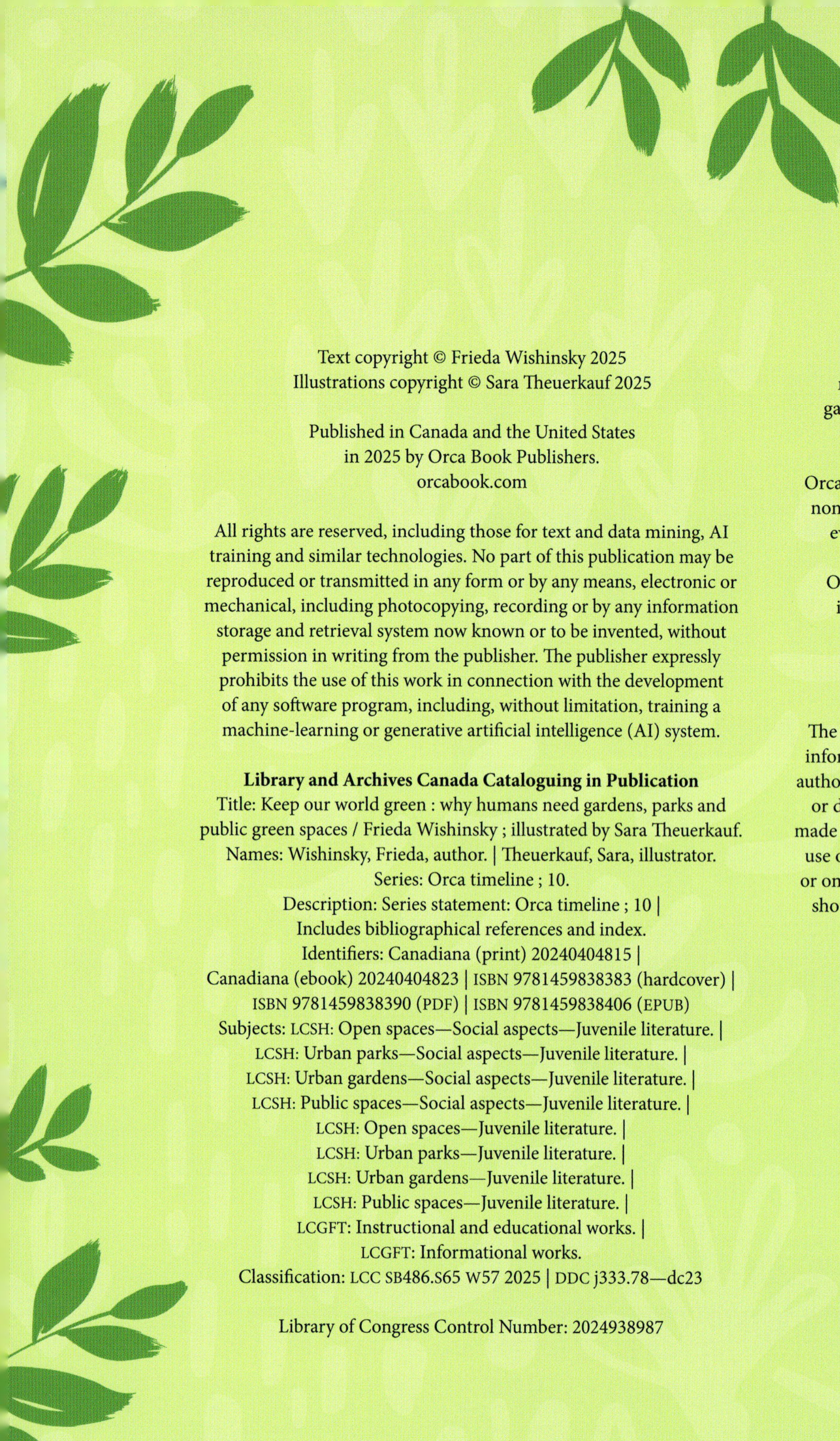

Published in Canada and the United States
in 2025 by Orca Book Publishers.
orcabook.com

Library and Archives Canada Cataloguing in Publication
Title: Keep our world green : why humans need gardens, parks and public green spaces / Frieda Wishinsky ; illustrated by Sara Theuerkauf.
Names: Wishinsky, Frieda, author. | Theuerkauf, Sara, illustrator.
Series: Orca timeline ; 10.
Description: Series statement: Orca timeline ; 10 |
Includes bibliographical references and index.
Identifiers: Canadiana (print) 20240404815 |
Canadiana (ebook) 20240404823 | ISBN 9781459838383 (hardcover) |
ISBN 9781459838390 (PDF) | ISBN 9781459838406 (EPUB)
Subjects: LCSH: Open spaces—Social aspects—Juvenile literature. |
LCSH: Urban parks—Social aspects—Juvenile literature. |
LCSH: Urban gardens—Social aspects—Juvenile literature. |
LCSH: Public spaces—Social aspects—Juvenile literature. |
LCSH: Open spaces—Juvenile literature. |
LCSH: Urban parks—Juvenile literature. |
LCSH: Urban gardens—Juvenile literature. |
LCSH: Public spaces—Juvenile literature. |
LCGFT: Instructional and educational works. |
LCGFT: Informational works.
Classification: LCC SB486.S65 W57 2025 | DDC j333.78—dc23

Library of Congress Control Number: 2024938987

Summary: Part of the nonfiction Orca Timeline series for middle-grade readers, this illustrated book examines parks, gardens and public green spaces throughout history and shares why it's important to protect them for future generations.

Orca Book Publishers is committed to reducing the consumption of nonrenewable resources in the production of our books. We make every effort to use materials that support a sustainable future.

Orca Book Publishers gratefully acknowledges the support for its publishing programs provided by the following agencies: the Government of Canada, the Canada Council for the Arts and the Province of British Columbia through the BC Arts Council and the Book Publishing Tax Credit.

Cover and interior artwork by Sara Theuerkauf.
Design by Dahlia Yuen.
Edited by Kirstie Hudson.

Printed and bound in South Korea.

28 27 26 25 • 1 2 3 4

In memory of my friend and fellow gardener Judy Illsley

As soon as you walk into Judy Illsley and John Crawford's garden in Scotland, you feel the magic of green space.

FRIEDA WISHINSKY

It's fun to meet friends in beautiful green city spaces.
WESTEND61/GETTY IMAGES

CONTENTS

INTRODUCTION

Why I Love Green Space

When I was a kid I lived in a six-story apartment building in New York City. My room faced an alley littered with garbage cans and rubble. Although the view from our apartment was dreary, I was lucky. I lived near a city park. Beyond the swings, past the water fountain, far from the sandbox, I discovered a world of boulders and trees. Sometimes my friends and I scrambled over rocks, acting out scenes from books about time travel and magic. Sometimes I played alone, imagining secret doors in trees that led to high mountains, lush forests and shimmering lakes.

When I went to high school, Fort Tryon Park came into my life. We'd moved north to a high-rise, but from our fifth-floor apartment I could see the densely planted, rolling hills of the park. I could see the Metropolitan Museum's cloisters, towering like an enchanted castle. I watched sunsets light up the sky. I marveled at the power of thunderstorms to play havoc with color, light and sound. I was mesmerized by the wildness of a winter storm. The park was a constant, shifting glorious show.

In those years I also loved spending time in that giant of parks, Central Park. I skirted it on weekends when I visited a museum on Fifth Avenue. I strolled through it and rowed on Central Park Lake. During my college years, I attended concerts and walked on paths in the park with friends.

Landscape architect Frederick Law Olmsted designed Central Park in New York City and many other parks across North America.
COURTESY OF THE US DEPARTMENT OF THE INTERIOR, NATIONAL PARK SERVICE, FREDERICK LAW OLMSTED NATIONAL HISTORIC SITE

Park Builder Frederick Law Olmsted

When we moved to Toronto, Central Park was still part of my life but only on trips to New York. Then I began to write kids' books. One day in the library I stumbled on a book about Frederick Law Olmsted, who had designed and helped build Central Park in the mid-1800s. I thought the park had always been there! It looked natural, not designed. I soon learned not only that Central Park had been planned but also that Olmsted and architect Calvert Vaux had won a contest to design the park. Olmsted even created a profession—landscape architecture. He believed that all people, rich and poor, young and old, deserved places of beauty and tranquility. He thought that parks were essential to soften the harshness of city life. He wanted newly arrived immigrants to experience something beautiful. He wanted them to know more than dismal, dirty streets and to breathe clean air. His beliefs, persistence and work resonated for me, a child of immigrants.

Olmsted created parks across North America and shaped each one to fit the existing land. He wanted each green space to be an island of beauty amid the clang and clamor of city life. And he not only built city parks but also was one of the first to champion establishing national parks like Yosemite in California. Olmsted believed that green spaces in every community should be preserved for generations to come.

Inspired, I wrote a picture-book biography about Olmsted, called *The Man Who Made Parks*. I wanted readers to not only appreciate his life and vision but to imagine how cold, empty and unhealthy our lives would be without green spaces. Sadly, since Olmsted's time the world has lost many forests, wetlands and trees to ***drought***, fire, war, industry and a disregard for our planet's warming climate. Today there's also recognition that the creation of green space displaced Indigenous people and other marginalized communities. We need to find ways to adapt and incorporate green spaces that are accessible to *everyone* wherever we live—city, suburb or rural community. Green space matters.

Frederick Law Olmsted and Calvert Vaux worked day and night to create their Greensward plan for the first North American city park. They hoped it would win them the job of designing Central Park, and it did.
GEOGRAPHICUS RARE ANTIQUE MAPS/ WIKIMEDIA COMMONS/PUBLIC DOMAIN

Central Park is fun all year round. In the fall you can enjoy the yellows, reds and oranges of the trees and plants. In warm weather, boating on the lake is a great thing to do.
(MAIN) ANDREW STRANOVSKY PHOTOGRAPHY/GETTY IMAGES; (INSET) HISHAM IBRAHIM/GETTY IMAGES

8000 BCE
The Fertile Crescent
2009
White House
Victory Garden
1300–TODAY
The three sisters

ONE

GREEN SPACE MATTERS

Green space is parks, gardens, nature reserves, farms, woods and meadows. It's the trees on a block. It's the plants in a window box. We need green space to grow food, stay healthy and feel happier. Green space helps us breathe cleaner air and drink safer water. If we live, go to school or work close to green space, we feel more optimistic and hopeful. And green space brings people together.

WIKIMEDIA COMMONS/PUBLIC DOMAIN

The Danger of One-Crop Farming

In the mid-1800s, when Ireland was a colony of the United Kingdom, it depended heavily on growing one crop—potatoes. When a destructive disease wiped out the potato plants, the ***tenant farmers*** starved. By 1852 more than one million Irish people died from starvation, and about a million more left Ireland for other countries. Growing only one crop year after year in the same spot robs the soil of nutrients, and the result is often ***blight*** or another disease attacking the entire crop.

We All Need to Eat c. 8000 BCE

The first humans on Earth were ***hunter-gatherers***. They followed animals from place to place and hunted them for food. About 10,000 years ago in the ***Fertile Crescent*** (a boomerang-shaped region of the Middle East), people also began to grow crops. Instead of chasing animal herds, they established communities, built homes and raised families in one place. They grew what worked well in their region and climate. They learned how to farm the land more efficiently, how to find water when it didn't rain and how to preserve food through drought, heat and cold. When they discovered that wild fruits like figs and berries were delicious, they planted fruit trees and berry bushes.

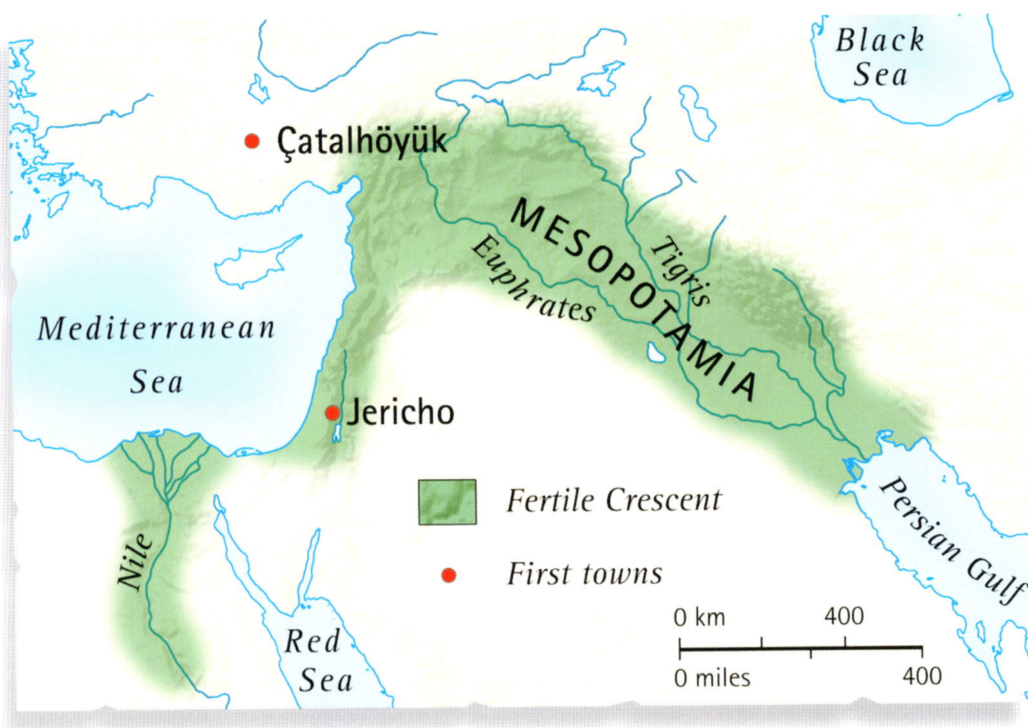

People first grew plants for food in the Fertile Crescent of Mesopotamia, a region that includes all of present-day Iraq and parts of Türkiye, Syria and Iran.
DORLING KINDERSLEY/GETTY IMAGES

The lush, fertile land of the Hevsel Gardens in Türkiye provides ideal growing conditions for food. This vital green space is designated a World Heritage site.
LUMOS AJANS/GETTY IMAGES

AT THE OTHER END OF THE WORLD

In another part of the world, Indigenous Peoples in the Americas also began growing crops. They too relied on local conditions, climate and shared knowledge to produce food. For example, when the Haudenosaunee planted the "three sisters" together—corn, beans and squash—they had fewer weeds, insects or animal pests. And the soil was better too.

COMMUNITIES CONNECT

As more people explored and traveled, they interacted with new communities and picked up new ideas. European colonizers in the Americas, for example, learned farming techniques from each region's Indigenous Peoples. Soon new foods appeared in new places. Different crops developed. Plants from all over the world provided medicine, shelter, dyes, fibers, clothing and soaps. Today, although the world is more connected than ever, growing healthy, productive plants is still key to everyone's survival.

Squash is a healthy vegetable that comes in many colors and shapes. This green squash is one of many varieties.
FRIEDA WISHINSKY

VICTORY GARDENS

During World Wars I and II, food was scarce and ***rationed*** by governments. Everyone was encouraged to plant gardens. In Canada, during World War I, the motto A Vegetable Garden for Every Home became popular, and expert gardeners visited schools to encourage gardening. In the United States, Charles Lathrop Pack organized the US National War Garden Commission, and then president Woodrow Wilson declared that "Food will win the war." During World War II, Australia began a Dig for Victory campaign. In the United Kingdom, unused land near railways, sports fields and golf courses was requisitioned for use as gardens. County Herb Committees were created to collect medicinal herbs. Even Buckingham Palace and Windsor Castle grew gardens. Recently there has been a renewed interest in victory gardens (often called "kitchen gardens"). In 2009 then First Lady Michelle Obama planted a kitchen garden on the White House lawn.

COURTESY OF THE IRWIN FAMILY

A Green Story

Families Who Hike Together...Have Fun

Lauren Irwin has always enjoyed hiking in California with her family. "It's something I loved as a kid," she said. "It's something I still love as I get older because it gives me time to think and makes me feel relaxed while doing something active." Lauren's mom, Amy, agrees. "Hiking has always brought me a sense of calm, peace, openness and freedom," she said.

We All Want to Be Healthy

City life can be hard on our health. Cities were already getting crowded in the late 1800s, when Frederick Law Olmsted, the designer of Central Park and many other parks, wrote, "The primary purpose of the Park is to provide the best practicable means of healthful recreation for the inhabitants of the city." Today more than 55 percent of the world's population lives in cities. If you live in an urban environment you're subjected to loud noises, hard concrete surfaces and stale, polluted air. That's not good for anyone.

WHAT IMPROVES LIFE IN A COMMUNITY?

Trees, parks and gardens improve life for people in all communities. According to studies from the Netherlands and Japan, walking in a forest or a park, digging in a garden or planting seeds is good for our health and helps us live longer. It's also about 5 to 10 degrees cooler under a tree. More trees means more shade. And with more shade, people have less exposure to hot, uncomfortable, unhealthy weather. Heat exposure can make people sick. As our climate warms up, shade will become increasingly important to everyone's health.

Trees and greenery also help clean the air. Cleaner air makes it easier to breathe. The three-year Chicago Urban Forest Climate Project in the early '90s showed how the city's more than 50 million trees cleaned the air of pollutants. Having fewer pollutants keeps more people healthy. Swedish scientist Roger Ulrich found that patients who looked out their hospital window at green space did better after surgery, used fewer pain medications and left the hospital sooner than patients who stared at a bare hospital wall.

> **"Nature in her green, tranquil woods heals and soothes all afflictions."**
>
> —JOHN MUIR, CONSERVATIONIST

We All Want to Feel Happy 2019

"Where flowers bloom, so does hope."

—LADY BIRD JOHNSON, FORMER FIRST LADY OF THE UNITED STATES

In 2019 researchers from Aarhus University in Denmark studied over a million people and discovered that children exposed to green space had a much lower risk of developing mental health issues during adolescence and adulthood. The researchers believed that access to exercise and interaction with people helped, as did having less noise and cleaner air. They also found that the longer the children were near green space, the healthier they felt. In 2021 the World Health Organization issued a report called *Green and Blue Spaces and Mental Health*, which also showed that being in nature improves a person's mood and mental health.

FEELING BETTER WHEREVER YOU LIVE

FRIEDA WISHINSKY

Every year volunteers plant masses of tulips in Central Park in the fall. After a bleak, gray city winter, many people are happy to see the tulips burst into bloom and fill the park with spring color.

FRIEDA WISHINSKY

The Japanese practice of shinrin-yoku, or forest bathing, encourages people to take a slow walk through a forest and inhale sweet forest smells. Forest bathing helps reduce blood pressure and alleviate depression.

MINT IMAGES/GETTY IMAGES

A 2019 study of 20,000 people in the United Kingdom showed that spending at least 120 minutes a week in nature improved people's sense of well-being.

CHERYL BRONSON/GETTY IMAGES

Parks and green space bring people together, especially in crowded, bustling cities. When the COVID-19 pandemic hit in 2020 and people were isolated, many became depressed. Parks became safe gathering places where people could talk, walk and feel close to nature and one another.

A Green Story
Healing Walks in Green Space
Toronto author and editor Bev Rosenbaum takes a walk almost every day. "I've found walking and hiking in nature helped me with the anxiety and depression I've struggled with off and on my whole life," she said. "I'm grateful to live in Toronto, which has a ravine system running all through the city and gorgeous parks that come with trails and streams."

1994
Joshua Tree National Park
C. 4000 BCE
Classical gardens of Suzhou
1545–TODAY
Orto Botanico di Padova
C. 3000 BCE
Egyptian gardens

TWO

GARDENS OF LONG AGO

Gardens have been important since ancient times. The Bible mentions the Garden of Eden, the beautiful setting for one of the oldest known stories. Pictures of gardens have been found on tomb walls from ancient Egypt. Garden remains were discovered while excavating the abandoned city of Petra, Jordan, where paths shaded by vines, date palms and grasses were enjoyed more than 2,000 years ago. Ancient manuscripts, including the Qur'an, the sacred text of the Islamic religion, depict beautiful gardens. What drew people long ago to create beautiful green spaces? Early gardens may give us some answers.

Ancient Egyptian Gardens c. 3000 BCE

Ancient Egyptian gardens are portrayed in pictures in pyramids and tombs that still stand in the desert today. The drawings show that the people living there more than 5,000 years ago planted fruits and vegetables. Eucalyptus trees and herbs were grown for cooking as well as to perfume the air. Fruits like the pomegranate were important for food, wine and medicine. Reeds made from ***papyrus*** plants were used for writing. Gardens and trees provided shade in the hot, dry climate. Egyptian gardens were also places in which to honor gods and enjoy beauty.

Pictures of early Egyptian gardens prove that humans created gardens long ago.
THE BRITISH MUSEUM/WIKIMEDIA COMMONS/PUBLIC DOMAIN

"To nurture a garden is to feed not just the body, but the soul. Show me your garden and I shall tell you what you are."
—ALFRED AUSTIN, ENGLISH POET

WHAT DID EGYPTIAN GARDENS LOOK LIKE?

The geometrically shaped Egyptian gardens usually grew around palaces and temples. Egyptians brought back plants from lands they'd conquered and planted them in their gardens. They filled their ponds with lotus flowers and fish. Trees were important to their daily lives and beliefs, and trees like the date palm were nurtured. Seating in the gardens was arranged beside a pond or in a pavilion.

Egyptians counted on the Nile River for much of the water they needed to grow food and garden. Since the Nile flooded regularly, the Egyptians created a system called basin irrigation—a network of earthen walls, dams and canals to channel the Nile's waters for their own use. Many elements of ancient Egyptian gardens, such as lotus blossoms, water lilies and ponds surrounded by fruit trees, are still used in modern gardens.

DAMS, DIKES AND AQUEDUCTS

Green spaces need water to grow and thrive. In ancient times people filled buckets with water from rivers, streams or wells to irrigate their crops. Ancient Egyptian and Chinese communities also built irrigation dams, dikes and water-storage facilities. Early Romans constructed ***aqueducts*** to bring water from the snow-covered mountains in the Alps to cities and towns below. Modern irrigation systems use some of these ancient techniques. Today the world faces less rainfall and more drought. We need to maintain and improve how we use our precious sources of water to grow crops and keep our world green.

The ancient gardens of Suzhou, China, are still visited today. The design of many new gardens shows the influence of the Suzhou gardens, which included pottery, trees, rocks and ponds.
MEIQIANBAO/SHUTTERSTOCK.COM

Classical Gardens of Suzhou c. 4000 BCE

There are gardens in eastern China that are at least 1,000 years old and still thriving today. The Suzhou gardens are found in Jiangsu province. They are an example of classical Chinese garden design that copies natural landscapes, but on a small scale. The gardens began as royal hunting grounds in the sixth century BCE, evolved into private gardens in the fourth century BCE and expanded into the 1700s when almost 200 of these classical gardens were built within the city walls. Today more than 50 of the Suzhou gardens survive.

The gardens reflect a love of a natural beauty and were inspired by poetry, philosophy and art. They have a free-flowing style and their design aims to balance the busy urban world with serene beauty. In creating an urban natural space, the gardens combine elements such as rocks, rivers, old trees, pottery and elegant bridges. Many of these garden ideas were handed down from generation to generation.

HOW ARE THE GARDENS USED TODAY?

The Suzhou gardeners continue to respect regional conditions and use local materials and plants. Although the gardens were begun long ago and have changed over time, they've maintained many of their earlier designs. Today 69 of the beautiful ancient gardens have been restored. Visitors from all over China and the world come to the gardens for festivals celebrating flowers, holidays and religious beliefs. Many Western gardens, such as the Huntington Botanical Gardens in Pasadena, California, have been influenced by the Suzhou gardens, and nine of the Suzhou gardens have been listed as ***UNESCO World Heritage sites***. Some have wonderful names, such as "The Mountain Villa with Embracing Beauty" and "The Lion Grove Garden."

Bonsai

Small and Beautiful

The Chinese were the first to cultivate ornamental and miniature natural scenery, around 2,000 years ago. This art was called penjing. When the practice reached Japan, it was renamed bonsai. By the 1600s the art of bonsai had become popular with wealthy Japanese people. By the turn of the 20th century, the art had spread around the globe. To make a bonsai, people place a plant in a small shallow container and prune and shape the stems and leaves in specific ways. Some bonsai plants and trees have survived as long as 800 to 1,000 years. Bonsai trees and landscapes continue to be appreciated and created all over the world.

ATIWICH KAEWCHUM/GETTY IMAGES

FRIEDA WISHINSKY

In the Middle Ages, people grew and studied medicinal plants in the Orto Botanico di Padova.
A. TOSINI - G AGOSTINI/WIKIMEDIA COMMONS/PUBLIC DOMAIN

Orto Botanico di Padova (Botanical Garden of Padua) 1545

Around the Middle Ages and earlier, the medicinal plants used by doctors were frequently misidentified and sometimes complete frauds, creating grave danger to people's health. In 1545 the medical school at the University of Padua requested that the Republic of Venice establish a garden where medicinal plants could be grown and students could learn to distinguish genuine medicinal plants from the false ones. The university asked the Benedictine monks of St. Justina to let them establish the garden on the grounds of the abbey. The Orto Botanico would advance knowledge in botany, medicine and pharmacy. After plants were grown and analyzed, the information would be shared. The monks agreed, and the garden was planted—but a new problem arose. Thieves stole valuable plants. To stop them, a wall was built around the garden. Over the years, more plants arrived at the garden from far-off places, especially those visited by Venetian traders and sailors.

The plants in the Orto Botanico di Padova still help heal people today.
EQROY/SHUTTERSTOCK.COM

THE ORTO BOTANICO TODAY

The Orto Botanico is thriving in its original location and is still used for studying and learning more about medicinal plants. It even looks similar to the way it was in the 1500s, with a circular central plot surrounded by a ring of water. It's been designated a UNESCO World Heritage site. This means the garden is considered an irreplaceable source of life and inspiration, a designation that helps prevent the garden's destruction. Some of today's healing gardens, such as the Royal Botanical Gardens in Burlington, Ontario, have been inspired by medieval gardens like the Orto Botanico.

Plants like mint and basil not only taste good but are good for you.
(LEFT) KARL TAPALES/GETTY IMAGES; (RIGHT) ANNASTILLS/GETTY IMAGES

MEDICINAL PLANTS HELP

Medicinal plants are grown and used all over the world. Many plants help with disease. Today they are analyzed by scientists to determine if and how they help with particular conditions or illnesses. Some commonly used medicinal plants are chamomile (for better sleep), peppermint (for upset stomachs), ginger (for nausea) and English lavender (also to improve sleep).

In the 1970s Chinese scientist Tu Youyou discovered that the compound artemisinin, obtained from artemisia plants, was effective in treating malaria. She won the 2015 Nobel Prize in Physiology or Medicine for her discovery. Scientists continue to study the 400-plus different species of plants used by Indigenous Peoples all over the world. Taxol, a medicine made from the bark of the Pacific yew tree in North America, is one of these plants, and it's now being used in cancer treatment.

The lives of people around the world changed when Chinese scientist Tu Youyou discovered that a compound in the artemisia plant could successfully treat malaria.
(MAIN) WIKIMEDIA COMMONS/PUBLIC DOMAIN; (INSET) ANTARESNS/GETTY IMAGES

Gardens of Versailles 1661

Throughout history royal, rich and powerful individuals and families have created magnificent and elaborate gardens. Some of the most famous are the gardens of the Palace of Versailles, built in 1661 by King Louis XIV, known as the Sun King. He decided to establish a magnificent palace with gardens to display his power and influence. The gardens were meant to impress not just the king's friends and his royal court but his enemies too, by showing he could tame nature. The palace and gardens were built on the grounds of the king's hunting lodge in Versailles, a town outside Paris, the capital of France.

"It's not a palace. It's an entire city. Superb in its size, superb in its matter."

—CHARLES PERRAULT, FRENCH FAIRY-TALE AUTHOR

The elaborate Palace of Versailles, built in the 1600s, has vast and magnificent green spaces.
KIRILL NEIEZHMAKOV/SHUTTERSTOCK.COM

HOW WERE THE VERSAILLES GARDENS BUILT?

The work on Versailles began under the guidance of landscape architect André Le Nôtre. His design was influenced by the classic French formal garden style emphasizing order and planting in rows. An innovative hydraulic system was created, which included pumps, aqueducts, ***reservoirs*** and artificial lakes. Thousands of men were recruited to help build the gardens. Many drained marshes for the extensive irrigation system.

Trees were hauled in from other regions in France. Meadows were dug up to build fountains, buildings and formal gardens. It took 40 years to complete the elaborate gardens, which covered about 2,000 acres (800 hectares). They contained about 370 statues, 50 fountains and 620 water jets, fed by more than 22 miles (35 kilometers) of water pipes. In 1979 the gardens were declared a UNESCO World Heritage site for their cultural importance during the 17th and 18th centuries. Today thousands of visitors continue to marvel at the grandeur and beauty of Versailles.

King Louis XIV added fabulous fountains and ornate sculptures to his Versailles gardens.
(MAIN) LOTSOSTOCK/SHUTTERSTOCK.COM;
(INSET) CARLO MARATTA/WIKIMEDIA COMMONS/
PUBLIC DOMAIN

Huntington Botanical Gardens 1904

If you make a fortune as the owner of railroads and real estate, what do you do with all that money? If you're Henry Huntington, you buy amazing art and create beautiful gardens. Huntington fell in love with the San Gabriel Valley in California and in 1903 bought a run-down citrus farm in nearby San Marino. In 1904 he hired William Hertrich, a young landscape architect, to turn the neglected old farm into a ***botanical garden***. Hertrich and his staff planted trees and vineyards and built greenhouses and an irrigation system. He grew a special garden for Huntington's wife, Arabella, so she could cut flowers for their mansion. Inspired by acclaimed artist Monet's gardens in Giverny (more about this in chapter 4), Hertrich created a lily pond as his first garden. He later planted rose and palm gardens, which helped spread those plants' popularity throughout California.

Joshua Tree National Park

1936

There are many cacti parks around the world, including in Monaco and Spain, but one of the most beautiful is Joshua Tree National Park in southern California. Two distinct desert ***ecosystems***, the Mojave and the Colorado, meet in Joshua Tree. Many plants and animals live in this stark and stunning place. Joshua Tree was designated a ***national monument*** in 1936 after wealthy widow Minerva Hoyt convinced then president Franklin D. Roosevelt of its distinctive beauty and environmental importance. In 1994 Joshua Tree was given national park status.

FRIEDA WISHINSKY

LET'S GROW CACTUS

In 1907 Hertrich suggested that Huntington establish a cactus garden. Cacti were suited to California's hot desert climate. At first Huntington said no. He'd once had a nasty encounter with a prickly cactus and didn't want to be near spiky plants again, but he eventually relented. The cactus garden grew larger and more varied each year. In 1912 Hertrich created a Japanese garden, with a traditional Japanese house and beautiful bridges. When Huntington died, his private garden was opened to the public. Hertrich stayed on as superintendent until his death in 1966. Today the Huntington Botanical Gardens feature 16 themed gardens, including magnificent Chinese gardens inspired by the Suzhou gardens. About 83,000 plants are grown, including many rare and endangered species. Thousands of people visit each year. The gardens are also a laboratory for research and conservation.

The Chinese Garden at the Huntington Botanical Gardens shows the influence of the ancient Suzhou gardens in China.

FRIEDA WISHINSKY

MATHEW BENJAMIN BRADY/WIKIMEDIA COMMONS/PUBLIC DOMAIN

Allerton and McBryde Gardens, Kauai, Hawaii 1938

Kauai, the most northerly and oldest Hawaiian Island, is also one of the wettest places on Earth. That makes it a good place for beautiful tropical gardens like the Allerton and the McBryde. In the 1880s the land was owned by Queen Emma of Hawaii. After her husband and son died, the queen planted rose apples, laurels, mangoes, bamboos, ferns and bougainvillea on the cliffs of the Lawai valley. The McBrydes took over the land and gardens, and then in 1938 they sold the land to Robert Allerton. Allerton added exotic plants and statues from his travels. The neighboring gardens grew and flourished.

"As long as you have a garden, you have a future, and as long as you have a future, you are alive."

—FRANCES HODGSON BURNETT, AUTHOR OF *THE SECRET GARDEN*

PRESERVING ENDANGERED PLANTS

In 1960 Allerton joined the National Tropical Botanical Garden (NTGB), an institution that works toward conserving tropical plants and restoring natural places. The NTGB helps preserve plants that might disappear unless we take special care of them.

Another NTGB garden in Kauai is Limahuli Garden and Preserve (which means "place of refuge") on the north shore. It's home to dozens of endangered plants that are not found anywhere else. It is also a place that practices biocultural conservation. That means it honors and adapts traditional Hawaiian ways of managing the land. Visitors to Limahuli discover that the Polynesian people who first settled the islands brought some of these plants with them in their canoes to honor their culture and help the settlers survive.

If you fly over the Allerton and McBryde Gardens, you see lush green fields surrounded by mountains covered in trees and plants.
CRAIG HINTON/SHUTTERSTOCK.COM

BILL WISHINSKY

A Green Story

In the Movies!

When I toured the beautiful Allerton and McBryde Gardens in 2018, I was amazed not only at the size of the ***Moreton Bay fig trees*** but also at discovering that one of these huge trees starred in *Jurassic Park*, a science fiction movie about dinosaurs brought back to life in modern times. Like many visitors to the gardens, I had my picture taken beside the thick roots of the tree. And for a few minutes, I closed my eyes and imagined being part of that thrilling 1993 movie too.

1847
Birkenhead Park,
England
2001
The Eden Project
1890
Yosemite
National Park
1858
Central Park,
New York

THREE

GREEN SPACE FOR EVERYONE

By the mid-1800s times were changing because of the Industrial Revolution. Immigrants flooded into countries like England and the United States. They worked long hours in crowded, unsanitary factories. Politicians and industrialists realized there was a need for places where workers and their families could relax. That led to the creation of the first city park—Birkenhead in England. Many cities followed Birkenhead's example.

> "Everybody needs beauty as well as bread."
>
> —JOHN MUIR, CONSERVATIONIST

A Cucumber a Day

Greenhouses are usually built with glass, and they use the warmth of the sun to grow plants indoors. The first greenhouse was created in Rome in the year 30 for Emperor Tiberius to grow cucumbers. He was told that eating a cucumber a day would improve his health. In the 17th century greenhouses became popular in Europe and the Americas. In 1787 then US president George Washington even built a greenhouse so he could grow pineapples to serve to his guests. The first modern greenhouse was built in the 1800s for French botanist Charles Lucien Bonaparte in Leiden, the Netherlands, to study medicinal plants. Universities and botanical gardens soon had greenhouses constructed in order to study and share exotic plants with the public. Today there are huge greenhouses like Thanet Earth in England, which produces about 400 million tomatoes, 30 million cucumbers and 24 million peppers each year.

Birkenhead Park, England 1847

From 1821 to 1851, when industries grew dramatically, workers filled factories and the population of Birkenhead grew. Many of the new workers were poor, laboring for long hours, and had little time or space to do anything else.

HOW WAS BIRKENHEAD DESIGNED?

Renowned architect and engineer Joseph Paxton was hired to transform the rough, neglected terrain in the growing city into a beautiful park. Birkenhead Park would provide a haven for people of all ages, backgrounds and incomes. Paxton built pathways and bridges. He planted trees and created terraces and hills. His design encouraged walkers to enjoy the views, trees and fresh air. It took five years to complete, but in 1847 about 10,000 people showed up on its opening day.

THE PEOPLE'S GARDEN

When young American Frederick Law Olmsted visited Birkenhead in 1850, he was enchanted by its beauty. He was also impressed that the park was built for everyone. A few years later, when Olmsted was commissioned to design New York City's Central Park, he looked to Birkenhead for inspiration and ideas.

When Birkenhead fell into disrepair in the late 20th century, the park was given a major facelift, and most of its original Victorian features were restored to their original beauty. Today Birkenhead, known as the People's Garden, has beautiful bridges, a boathouse and woodlands. It continues to welcome everyone in the community, regardless of age, background or ability.

Today the farms, hills and valleys in the Lake District look a lot like they did a hundred years ago thanks to author Beatrix Potter, who saved them from development.

ALEX_WEST/GETTY IMAGES

Beatrix Potter

How Peter Rabbit Saved Green Space

Beatrix Potter, the author of over 25 children's books including *The Tale of Peter Rabbit*, was not only passionate about writing and illustrating but was also a dedicated farmer and conservationist. She loved the rolling hills and valleys of England's Lake District and used the money she earned as a creator of children's literature to buy over 4,000 acres (16 square kilometers) of hill farm property. She didn't want the land to be destroyed for factories or industry. Potter died in 1943 but gifted her many properties to the English National Trust. She wanted everyone to be able to enjoy its beauty. The land is now part of ***Lake District National Park***, England's most scenic and popular reserve.

Civil rights activist and educator Maritcha Remond Lyons lived in Seneca Village before the land was taken over to become part of Central Park.

HARRY A. WILLIAMSON PHOTOGRAPH COLLECTION/WIKIMEDIA COMMONS/PUBLIC DOMAIN

Central Park, New York 1858

When young Frederick Law Olmsted visited Birkenhead Park in England in 1850, he was amazed to walk around a beautiful public park in the heart of a busy city. Little did he know that a few years later he'd be offered the job of building and designing a public park out of 840 acres (3.4 square kilometers) of rocky marshland in the middle of New York City. The development of Central Park, like Birkenhead, arose from the influx of immigrants. The newcomers worked and lived in crowded, unsanitary conditions. They needed green space in which to relax, enjoy the outdoors and breathe fresh air.

HOW LONG DID IT TAKE TO BUILD CENTRAL PARK?

It took more than 15 years to complete Central Park. Sixteen hundred people were displaced to build the park, including the residents of Seneca Village, a mainly Black community that had been there since 1825. The city was able to take over private land for the park as long as they paid the landowners, although many said their land was undervalued. Olmsted and his partner, architect Calvert Vaux, had to deal with corrupt and interfering politicians. The Civil War and the complicated task of moving rocks, draining swamps, installing irrigation and planting trees slowed them down too.

Soon other cities clamored for their own city parks. In the years that followed, Olmsted built parks all over the United States and Canada. In 1865 he also proposed that the stunning area around Yosemite, California, be designated a national park. It took almost 30 years, but with the support of other environmental champions like John Muir, Yosemite became the third US national park in 1890.

A Green Story

Green Stories...for City Kids

Author Jennifer Baum recalls happy times spent in Central Park. "I grew up a block and a half away from Central Park," she said. "It was like my own backyard. It made life more livable in cement- and concrete-heavy New York City." Educator Miriam Koral remembers the joy she had as a kid playing in Inwood Hill, a large, sprawling park in northern Manhattan. "Inwood [Hill] Park had natural hills ideal for roller skating or catching fireflies in the summer and sledding down in the winter," she said.

RUBIN KORAL

Central Park welcomes everyone to relax, enjoy nature and get away from the buzz of a busy city.
PAWEL.GAUL/GETTY IMAGES

Cat Ba National Park, Vietnam 1986

The beautiful Cat Ba Archipelago in Vietnam has been settled, farmed and fished for hundreds of years. It's also been the site of battles and lookout spots during wars that forced residents to hide in local caves. But finally, in the 1980s, there was peace in Vietnam, and peace brought change and renewal. In 1986 Cat Ba National Park was established. By the 1990s roads were built, electricity was introduced, dams were constructed and hotels popped up, drawing tourists to this diverse and magnificent landscape. Today people kayak and take boat cruises in the park. They can hike through forests, ride mountain bikes, swim around Monkey Island (one of the 367 limestone islands in the Cat Ba Archipelago) and explore hidden caves.

The Eden Project: Our Place in Nature

In the late 1990s a small group of environmentalists in Cornwall, England, decided to create a unique place that would explore the human connection to nature. By 2001 they'd bought a steep clay pit that had no soil or water. There they built giant conservatories and buildings inspired by nature. They filled them with diverse plants, set them in soil made from waste materials and let the rain water them. The Eden Project's rainforest *biome* shows how rainforests cool the earth. Despite flooding in 2010, the Eden Project has thrived and expanded to other locations around the world. Eden Projects International plans to open new projects in the United Kingdom, Colombia and Australia.

A1PERSONAGE/WIKIMEDIA COMMONS/PUBLIC DOMAIN

You'll see many jagged limestone islands if you travel by boat in Cat Ba National Park in Vietnam.

VITHUN KHAMSONG/GETTY IMAGES

CAT BA BIOSPHERE RESERVE

Cat Ba National Park is not just a beautiful place. Its ***mangrove trees***, with their dense roots and ***seagrasses***—flowering plants that live underwater—bind the soil and are key to preventing ***erosion***. Its tropical forests, wetlands and coral reefs are important ecosystems that encourage ***biodiversity***—the variety of life in all forms, from bacteria and animals to plants and trees. Forests and wetlands take in and store carbon—too much carbon contributes to climate change and hotter weather. Animals like the rare ***golden-headed langur*** and dozens more are only found in Cat Ba. The park gives threatened species a chance to avoid going extinct. It is a core part of the Cat Ba Archipelago, which, in order to help protect its many diverse animals, plants and water features, was in 2004 declared a ***biosphere reserve*** by the United Nations Educational, Scientific and Cultural Association (UNESCO) in its Man and the Biosphere program.

1883
Monet's
Giverny garden
2013
Braiding Sweetgrass,
Robin Wall Kimmerer
BRAIDING
SWEETGRASS
1992
Central Garden,
Getty Center
LEAVE ME THE
BIRDS & THE BEES
1970
"Big Yellow Taxi,"
Joni Mitchell

FOUR

GREEN SPACE INSPIRES ART, MUSIC AND LITERATURE

Theodor Seuss Geisel, better known as children's book author and illustrator Dr. Seuss, loved nature and trees. His 1971 book *The Lorax*, about the damage people do to the natural world, was inspired by the Monterey cypress tree. Geisel lived in La Jolla, California, and could see the cypress from his window. Like Geisel, many artists, writers and composers have been inspired by and celebrated green space in their work.

People flock to Giverny, France, to see artist Claude Monet's Japanese-style green bridge and his gardens.
METROPOLITAN MUSEUM OF ART/WIKIMEDIA COMMONS/PUBLIC DOMAIN

Monet's Giverny 1883

Forty miles from the bustling city of Paris there's a small village called Giverny. In 1883 artist Claude Monet saw the village from a train and liked it so much, he decided it would be a good place to rent a house and start a garden. He'd always loved flowers and was soon swapping seeds and cuttings with friends in the village. By 1890 Monet's reputation as an artist had grown so much that he had enough money to buy the house and nearby land in Giverny. He also hired full-time gardeners to help him expand the garden that he had started when he was renting the house, transforming a nearby swamp into a pond with water lilies. Inspired by his love of Japanese art, he designed an elegant Japanese-style green bridge over the pond.

"My garden is my most beautiful masterpiece. I can only draw what I see."

—CLAUDE MONET, PAINTER

Frida Kahlo

Flowers in Her Hair, Flowers in Her Garden

Casa Azul, the home of renowned Mexican artist Frida Kahlo, is lush with palm trees and local plants. Kahlo, who was badly injured in a streetcar accident in 1925, spent much of her time surrounded by the flowers and plants in her gardens, which in turn inspired her art. The gardens are filled with native and tropical plants, and its pathways allowed Kahlo to travel through them in a wheelchair. She died in 1954. Many of the plants and trees that gave Kahlo joy still grow in Casa Azul today, which welcomes about 25,000 visitors a month.

ROSES AND PEONIES

Giverny gave Monet endless joy and became the subject of many of his stunning paintings. "The richness I achieve comes from nature, the source of my inspiration," he said. Monet understood how gardens can lift your spirit. He said that when he was a child, green space helped him get through unhappy times. "I perhaps owe having become a painter to flowers," he wrote.

Monet was proud of his vibrant roses, geraniums, lavender, pansies, irises and peonies. He loved hosting parties and picnics and inviting other artists to enjoy his garden. One of Monet's friends, American painter John Singer Sargent, was so impressed he even painted a picture of Monet in his garden. Today Giverny continues to charm thousands of visitors, who flock to see the gardens Monet created many years ago.

A Green Story

Born in a Forest House

French-born artist Genevieve Jost moved to Quebec in 1967. Her paintings reflect her love of green space. "My father was a ranger, I was born in a forest house—perhaps that determined my love for nature," she said. "I am in love with green color, and in each of my paintings there is a touch of green. I love particularly trees. I talk to them, they are like my friends, and I am never happier than in a forest."

Georgia O'Keeffe's Abiquiú Garden 1945

The day she first visited New Mexico in 1929, American artist Georgia O'Keeffe fell in love with its stark, eye-catching desert landscape. That landscape influenced much of her art. She moved to New Mexico permanently in 1949, where she lived in two homes, Ghost Ranch and Abiquiú. Although she spent many days on remote Ghost Ranch, observing and painting desert plants, she often returned to Abiquiú, where she grew a garden. She started the garden so she wouldn't have to leave her property to buy vegetables like lettuce, chard and kale, and fruits like pears, peaches and apples. She also planted beautiful flowers like lilacs and daylilies. But O'Keeffe didn't nurture the garden alone. She hired Estibin Suazo to help her. Not only did he take care of the flowers and plants, but he taught his grandchildren to care for the garden too. Even when O'Keeffe lost her vision later in life she loved wandering through her garden, staying on the paths so she wouldn't trample any of the plants.

> **"If you look the right way, you can see that the whole world is a garden."**
>
> —FRANCES HODGSON BURNETT, AUTHOR OF *THE SECRET GARDEN*

LEARNING AND SHARING

Today the Abiquiú garden is part of the Georgia O'Keeffe Museum. Both the museum and the Santa Fe Botanical Garden bring in local high school students to learn about organic gardening. They also learn about O'Keeffe's art. At the end of the growing season the students harvest the produce and share it with their families and local food banks.

Central Garden, Getty Center 1992

"Always changing, never twice the same" is the mantra of the whimsical, innovative and colorful garden designed by artist Robert Irwin for the Getty Center, a campus of the Getty Museum in Los Angeles. Irwin calls the Central Garden a "sculpture in the form of a garden aspiring to be art." Irwin began creating it in 1992. Hiring him was an unusual choice. He wasn't a gardener or a landscape designer. He began his career as a painter, but in 1966 he decided to expand into other areas of art like architecture and sculpture.

When Irwin was hired, the Getty Center's renowned architect, Richard Meir, was against his selection. Meir didn't like Irwin's unusual plans and lack of garden experience. But Irwin was determined to create something unique and make a living work of art. He realized that you can make plans, but nature will often do something you never expected, and something that's often more wonderful than you imagined.

NATURE DESIGNS

Irwin also knew he needed to learn more about plants, trees and flowers. He enlisted the help of master gardener Jim Duggan. Both men believed that going through the garden should be an adventure for everyone who visits. At first the completed Central Garden, covering 134,000 square feet (12,449 square meters) was controversial, but today visitors delight in the unusual combination of shape, light, form and color. And many, like Irwin, also appreciate that in the end, nature will be the ultimate artist and will often create the unexpected.

The gardens at the Getty Center in Los Angeles are a work of art. Their colors and plants change in every season.
(LEFT) BKINGFOTO/SHUTTERSTOCK.COM; (RIGHT) CERI BREEZE/SHUTTERSTOCK.COM

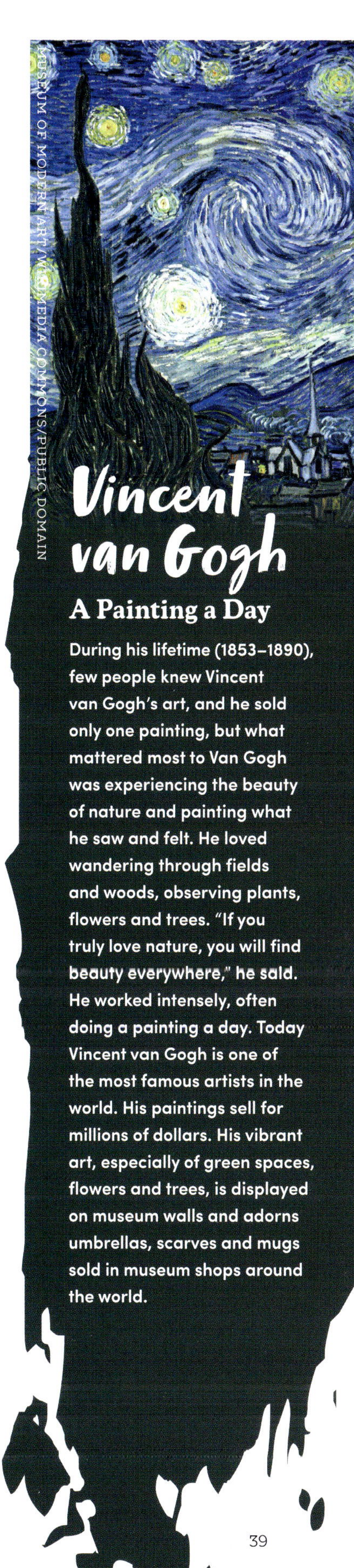

MUSEUM OF MODERN ART/WIKIMEDIA COMMONS/PUBLIC DOMAIN

Vincent van Gogh

A Painting a Day

During his lifetime (1853–1890), few people knew Vincent van Gogh's art, and he sold only one painting, but what mattered most to Van Gogh was experiencing the beauty of nature and painting what he saw and felt. He loved wandering through fields and woods, observing plants, flowers and trees. "If you truly love nature, you will find beauty everywhere," he said. He worked intensely, often doing a painting a day. Today Vincent van Gogh is one of the most famous artists in the world. His paintings sell for millions of dollars. His vibrant art, especially of green spaces, flowers and trees, is displayed on museum walls and adorns umbrellas, scarves and mugs sold in museum shops around the world.

I love funky jewelry—and so does this giant wooden troll!
BILL WISHINSKY

Trolls Like Green Space Too

Danish sculptor and artist Thomas Dambo, from fairy-tale writer Hans Christian Andersen's hometown of Odense, had a great idea. Why not build giant trolls out of recycled material (mostly wood) and set them up around the world to promote the importance of preserving and appreciating green space? Dambo's first giant troll, Hector el Protector, was made for a site in Puerto Rico in 2014, and everyone fell in love with the huge, friendly troll. Dambo's trolls inspire us to look at trash in a different way and appreciate the natural world. So far there are 100 trolls traveling to different botanical gardens, zoos or other community places all over the world. And more trolls are coming. Maybe to a city near you.

Say It in Words

Some writers have described how calming and uplifting it is to walk in the woods. Others have focused on the harm done to green space by the chemicals and pollutants we use.

XRRR/GETTY IMAGES

William Wordsworth (1770–1850), a great English poet, often wrote about his love of the natural world. One of his most famous poems, "I Wandered Lonely as a Cloud," describes how he felt in a field of daffodils.

ROCTER/GETTY IMAGES

American writer **Henry David Thoreau** (1817–1862) described his experiences living alone in a cabin in the woods in *Walden; or, Life in the Woods*. His work influenced other writers and readers to observe the world around them.

TZAHIV/GETTY IMAGES

E.B. White (1899–1985), author of the classic children's book *Charlotte's Web*, carried Thoreau's *Walden* everywhere. His work was also inspired by scientist and environmentalist Rachel Carson, whose book *Silent Spring* discussed the harmful effects of ***pesticides*** such as DDT, a chemical that was sprayed on plants to control insects.

EFOART/GETTY IMAGES

Botanist and writer **Robin Wall Kimmerer** (1953–) explores the relationship between humans and plants in her bestselling book *Braiding Sweetgrass: Indigenous Wisdom, Scientific Knowledge and the Teachings of Plants*. "Knowing that you love the earth changes you, activates you to defend and protect and celebrate," she writes.

DENISTANGNEYJR/GETTY IMAGES

Louise Erdrich (1954–) set her book *The Painted Drum* among trees and mountains in New Hampshire.

ROBERTO MOIOLA/SYSAWORLD/GETTY IMAGES

Gary Paulsen (1939–2021) often wrote about how teens are changed by experiences with nature. In his 1986 young-adult classic *Hatchet*, Paulsen tells the story of a Canadian boy who is forced to survive in the wilderness after a plane crash. Paulsen wrote from his own experiences as a trapper, hunter and dogsledder who found strength and comfort in nature.

REBECCA UPJOHN

A Green Story

Rebecca Upjohn

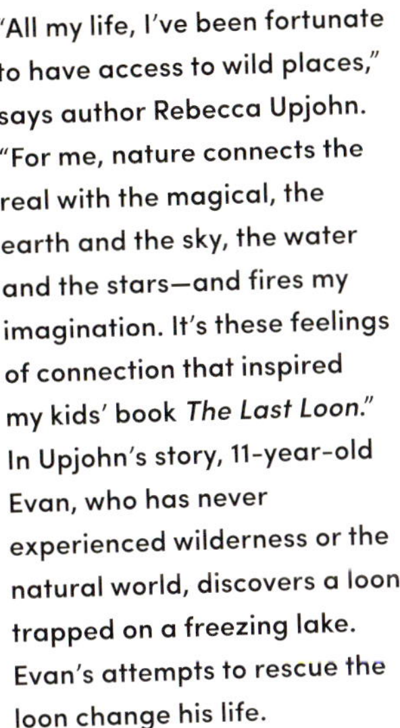

"All my life, I've been fortunate to have access to wild places," says author Rebecca Upjohn. "For me, nature connects the real with the magical, the earth and the sky, the water and the stars—and fires my imagination. It's these feelings of connection that inspired my kids' book *The Last Loon*." In Upjohn's story, 11-year-old Evan, who has never experienced wilderness or the natural world, discovers a loon trapped on a freezing lake. Evan's attempts to rescue the loon change his life.

Say It in Music

Many composers of classical music have been inspired by the sounds of nature, such as the songs of birdsong, the buzz of bees or wind whistling through leaves. Others have been influenced by the beauty of such things as walking in a forest or being surrounded by a meadow of flowers. Composers of contemporary music have warned us of the dangers of losing our green spaces.

A trio fills a French garden with music.
FRIEDA WISHINSKY

Nature can inspire you to make beautiful music.
LOURDES BALDUQUE/GETTY IMAGES

You can almost hear the colors change in Vivaldi's Four Seasons *concertos.*
(LEFT) JITTAWIT.21/GETTY IMAGES;
(RIGHT) STUDIO LIGHT AND SHADE/GETTY IMAGES

PLAYING FOR THE PLANET

Around 1720 **Antonio Vivaldi** composed his beautiful *Four Seasons* concertos. He was inspired by how nature changes with each season.

Antonín Dvořák's "Silent Woods," from *From the Bohemian Forest*, op. 68, no. 5, composed in 1883, is like a musical walk through a forest. Nature was important to the composer, who took daily walks, often with his children. He also gardened, planted trees and loved listening to birdsong.

TREVOR WILLIAMS/GETTY IMAGES

MARIUSZ_PRUSACZYK/GETTY IMAGES

TERESA KOPEC/GETTY IMAGES

Amy Beach (1867–1944) began playing piano when she was four and performed on stage at 16. Much of her work, such as the musical pieces "Fire-Flies" and "In Autumn," were inspired by nature. Beach loved composing surrounded by green space at the MacDowell Colony, an artists' retreat in New Hampshire, where she also mentored many young female composers.

Gabriela Lena Frank was born in 1972 with profound hearing loss. When she was four, she heard sounds for the first time after being given hearing aids. "The air just came alive when they turned it on," she said. Frank has gone on to have a successful career as a composer. Her music honors her Peruvian-Chinese-Jewish-Lithuanian roots, and her composition *Milagros* is inspired by the Amazon wetlands in Peru.

Much of modern French composer **Olivier Messiaen's** music is inspired by birdsong. His work reminds us of a summer day. He called birds the earth's "first musicians." After his death in 1992, a mountain peak in Utah was named after the composer to honor his love of nature.

Ludwig van Beethoven

A Passion for Green: A Walk in the Woods

Many people consider Ludwig van Beethoven (1770–1827) one of the greatest composers who ever lived. Some of Beethoven's music was inspired by nature and the outdoors. Escaping the busy, polluted city of Vienna, he found peace and solace in the countryside. He often would take a notebook along on his walks and jot down musical ideas. "How happy I am to be able to walk among the shrubs, the trees, the woods, the grass and the rocks—no one can love the countryside more than I do—for the woods, the trees, and the rocks give a man the inspiration he needs," he wrote.

> **"The earth has music for those who listen."**
> —UNKNOWN

It's fun to play music surrounded by beautiful green space!
KYOTOKUSHIGE/GETTY IMAGES

SINGING FOR THE PLANET

Canadian musician and songwriter **Joni Mitchell** was visiting Hawaii in the 1970s when she looked out of her hotel room. She saw beautiful green mountains in the distance and a parking lot below her window. The two views inspired Mitchell to write "Big Yellow Taxi," a song about how humans destroy the environment. The song is still popular and has been covered by hundreds of other artists.

Inspired by watching and thinking about trees and listening to birds in his own yard, popular songwriter **Brian Wilson**, part of the rock band the Beach Boys, co-wrote the song "A Day in the Life of a Tree" in 1971 about a single tree. It tells the story of the tree in its own words and what happens to it because of pollution. It's on the Beach Boys album *Surf's Up*.

Michael Jackson's "Earth Song" song came out in 1995 and mourns humanity's greed and the destruction of the planet. The music video incorporates dramatic and heart-wrenching scenes of trees and creatures around the world and how they are being brutally destroyed by industry and climate change.

The rap song "S.O.S (Mother Nature)" from 2020 highlights the devastation humans have caused to natural spaces through ***deforestation***, pollution and climate change. Singer **will.i.am** says we need to do something now to protect our fragile planet.

We need more trees and less concrete. We need more green space and less pollution!
(TOP) XIJIAN/GETTY IMAGES; (BOTTOM) SHAUNL/GETTY IMAGES

2012
Waldorf Astoria
Hotel apiary
2004
Ría Celestún
Biosphere Reserve
1830
Invention of
the lawn mower
1861
Tijuca Forest,
Rio de Janeiro

FIVE

GREEN SPACE IN DANGER

Over the last 100 years, we've moved from a society where most people farmed to one where most people live or work in cities. Green spaces such as forests and wetlands have been cut back to build factories, sprawling housing developments and gigantic ***industrial farms***.

"Look after the land and the land will look after you, destroy the land and it will destroy you."

—PROVERB

Perfect-looking lawns often require chemicals that are harmful to our environment and our health.
JAMESBREY/GETTY IMAGES

The Perfect Lawn 500

In medieval times, from around 500 until the 1400s, in what is now Europe and Britain, people created open grassy areas to help them see who was approaching their castle. Meanwhile, in villages and towns, a grassy space called a ***village common*** was mostly set aside for animals to graze. By the 16th century wealthy landowners in France and England had created fashionable lawns that had to be cut with hand tools. The invention of the lawn mower in the mid-1800s and the popularity of the Scottish games of golf and lawn bowling spread the idea of a manicured lawn much further. Many homeowners wanted neat, tidy, weed-free lawns. Unfortunately, perfect lawns are hard to maintain without adding harmful chemicals.

BUILDING BIGGER

Around the same time, industry expanded, and as it did, green spaces were destroyed. The loss of green space affected animal and plant species, leaving them with fewer places where they could thrive or even survive. By the 1920s small farms began to make way for large industrial farms, which used more fuel and chemical fertilizers to produce large harvests of crops and animals. Chemicals often polluted the water and air.

Green Spaces vs. Cities 2022

Since 1980, in a period of rapid economic growth, development in Seoul, the capital of South Korea, destroyed much of the area's green space—less than 4 percent of the city was park or green space by 2022. This prompted Seoul mayor Oh Se-hoon to acknowledge the problem, and in 2023 he announced that projects were underway to restore and create green space to transform Seoul into a place "where all citizens can stroll around the downtown and everything they see is trees and forests." It's a challenge, as so much green space has been lost in the city. One project saw a sky garden built on a former inner-city highway in Seoul, and it is now home to more than 24,000 native plants.

ADOPT A PLANT!

Korean visual artist Baik Soo-hye has rescued more than 300 plants from construction sites, garbage dumps, cracks in concrete pavement and other sites across Seoul. She nurses them back to health and takes care of them in what she calls her "plant kindergarten." Then she tells each plant's "story" and invites people, via social media, to adopt it. Many of the new "plant parents" are in their 20s and 30s. The response has been so good that Baik decided to host a "graduation ceremony" and invited people to her apartment to see the plants available in person and exchange ideas about houseplants.

The Giant Tijuca Forest, Brazil

In 1861 Brazilian emperor Dom Pedro II established the Tijuca Forest in Rio de Janeiro in order to reforest the land after forests had been cut down to make space for sugarcane and coffee plantations. Today it's still one of the world's biggest and most beautiful urban forests.

Climate Changes Everything 2012

Our climate is changing. In the last 20 years, we've experienced more and more extreme weather events. Violent storms are becoming more common. Hurricanes devastate property and hurt people. Heat, floods and drought threaten lives and the survival of trees and plants in vital green spaces. As Mark O'Callaghan, an educator and guide at the National Botanic Gardens of Ireland in Dublin, puts it, "If plants disappeared, we'd disappear too."

WETLANDS MATTER

In 2012 Hurricane Sandy hit the east coast of the United States. It caused devastation in 24 states, claimed the lives of over 200 people in eight countries and cost billions of dollars in damage. But it could have been worse. In 2017 a study in *Scientific Reports* found that mangrove trees, which grow in wetland swamps and trap water like natural sponges, helped reduce flooding, erosion and the loss of property by about US $625 million.

Wetlands also provide us with fish, shellfish, blueberries, cranberries and wild rice. Some wetlands supply plants for medicines. Animals and reptiles live in wetlands. Birds feed, nest and rest there. Wetlands improve our natural water quality. But swamps and wetlands are disappearing as more and more land gets developed.

Ría Celestún
Wetland in the Yucatan

The fishing village of Celestún is the gateway to a vast wetland in Mexico's Yucatán. It's home to over 304 resident and migrating bird species, including flamingos, and more than 587 plants species and trees, including mangroves. In 2004 the wetland was declared a biosphere reserve. Despite this important designation, Ría Celestún and other precious wetlands around the world are constantly being threatened by politicians and developers who want to destroy green spaces to expand industry.

(MAIN) FRIEDA WISHINSKY; (INSET) BMCHURCH/GETTY IMAGES

All Kinds of Forests

There are different kinds of forests. Each helps sustain life for people, animals and insects.

Rainforests can be tropical or temperate, but both get a lot of rain. They are lush, wet landscapes.

Mossy green cloud forests are a type of rainforest found at high altitudes. Clouds cover them even in the dry season.

Old-growth forests, usually found in wilderness areas, support diverse plants and animal life and feature stands of large, old trees. They haven't been disturbed by logging or fire.

Boreal forests are found in northern regions of the planet and typically have coniferous trees (trees with cones and needles rather than leaves).

> **"We must protect the forests for our children, grandchildren and children yet to be born. We must protect the forests for those who can't speak for themselves, such as the birds, animals, fish and trees."**
>
> —QWATSINAS (HEREDITARY CHIEF EDWARD MOODY), NUXALK NATION

HOTTEST YEAR EVER—SO FAR

Using data from weather stations and ships at sea, NASA's Goddard Institute for Space Studies confirmed that 2023 was the hottest year since 1880. That heat threatened many species and increased the number of wildfires, floods and drought conditions around the world. Climate change also affects biodiversity. Elizabeth Maruma Mrema, executive secretary of the United Nations Convention on Biological Diversity, notes that as the climate heats up, we lose many animals, plants and trees that are important to our survival.

Bees and Butterflies 9000 BCE

Ancient cave paintings show people climbing to reach wild beehives and prove that humans have loved the sweet taste of bee honey for more than 11,000 years. Art from 4,500 years ago shows ancient Egyptians made artificial hives out of pottery vessels or woven straw baskets. According to archaeologists, the Hebrews loved honey so much they even had hives in the middle of their cities in the mid-10th century BCE.

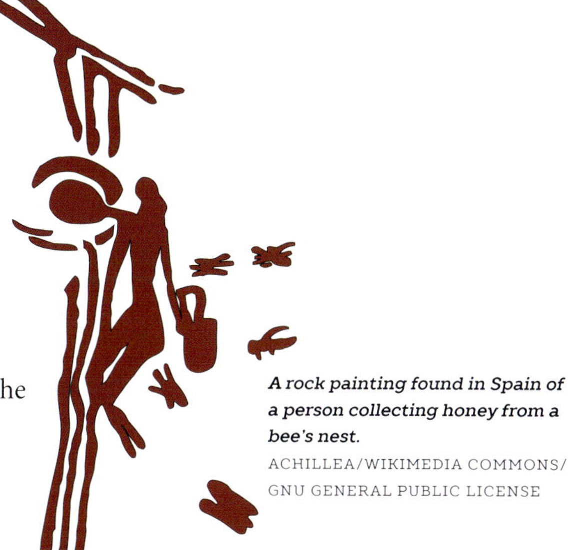

A rock painting found in Spain of a person collecting honey from a bee's nest.

ACHILLEA/WIKIMEDIA COMMONS/ GNU GENERAL PUBLIC LICENSE

Give Bees a Chance

Since 2008, to boost the dwindling bee population, beehives have been established in elegant hotels around the world. Bees are thriving on the rooftop of the Waldorf Astoria in New York City. More than 300,000 bees in six active hives call that fancy hotel home and are busy making honey 20 stories up. The elegant Baur au Lac in Zurich has a beehive that looks like a miniature version of the hotel, while Toronto's Shangri-La Hotel has a luxury "condo" known as the Bee Wall, made of wax secreted by some 50,000 honeybees, on its third-floor terrace. The sunny second floor of Vancouver's Fairmont Waterfront hotel hosts a daily Bee and Garden tour. Foods that require pollination are featured on its menu with the words *Give Bees a Chance*. A popular dish is the Bee's Knees sundae, which features rooftop honey caramel, salted-honey pecan and torched honey marshmallow.

Beehives are being established in many urban locations such as hotels.

(LEFT) BUSÀ PHOTOGRAPHY/GETTY IMAGES; (RIGHT) LIA BUFFA/GETTY IMAGES

WHAT'S THE BUZZ?

Over time people realized that bees not only make delicious honey but are responsible for pollinating much of our fruit, nuts and vegetables. Without them our food supply would be in trouble. Seventy of the top 100 food crops are pollinated by bees. In her 2014 book *Taming Wildflowers,* Miriam Goldberger says that bees are the most efficient of all ***pollinators***, and native bees do an even better job at pollinating than imported honeybees.

But in the last 20 years, bees around the world have been dying because of pollution and chemical pesticides and ***fungicides***. Researchers have found more than 150 ***toxic*** chemicals in bee pollen. The destruction of green spaces also makes it tougher for bees to survive. As bee habitat shrinks and concrete takes its place, bees lose the environment they need to thrive.

SURVIVE AND THRIVE

Butterflies also pollinate plants. But butterflies have been experiencing many of the same problems as bees—a loss of green space and fewer of the plants they like to pollinate. Weather and climate have also disrupted butterflies' migration paths. The population of monarch butterflies has declined by more than 80 percent in the last 20 years.

Providing urban spaces filled with native wildflowers and converting lawns into meadows with native plants such as black-eyed Susans, Canadian goldenrod, New England asters, purple coneflowers, willow trees and a variety of fruit trees and shrubs will help. Plants like milkweed, daisies, lavender and zinnias will attract butterflies.

A Green Story

A Butterfly Is Born!

Winnipeg writer Harriet Zaidman didn't realize a milkweed plant was growing close to her lush rhubarb plants in her garden until her granddaughter noticed a ***chrysalis*** forming on a leaf. Over the next few days, the family observed the changes in the chrysalis. They knew that a butterfly would soon emerge from the chrysalis. And when it did, it was a magical moment! Their green space had become the birthplace for a beautiful butterfly.

HARRIET ZAIDMAN

1929
Shelburne Bridge of Flowers
TODAY–2040
Urban Forest Visual map, Melbourne
Corymbia Flowering Gum
Age: Mature
Click HERE to Email this tree
RADISHES
2008
Svalbard Global Seed Vault
2005
First "parklet," San Francisco

SIX

GREAT GREEN IDEAS

Many communities have created innovative, inclusive and unique green space projects. Some green spaces began with the vision of one or two people. After they found others to help, they established beautiful green spaces, sometimes out of ugly or abandoned areas. Often they had to persuade politicians and corporations to go along with their idea.

> **"To plant a garden is to dream of tomorrow."**
>
> —AUDREY HEPBURN, ACTRESS

We Can All Make a Difference 1929

There's a lot we can all do to expand and protect our green spaces. No matter how old we are or where we live, we can share our love of the natural world. We can speak up when green space is threatened or destroyed. We can start our own gardens or help a neighbor, relative or friend garden.

FRIEDA WISHINSKY

BRIDGE OF FLOWERS

In 1929, Shelburne Falls, Massachusetts, resident Antoinette Burnham's home overlooked a rusty old trolley bridge. One day Burnham decided that turning the bridge into a green space would improve everyone's lives in her community. So Burnham and her friends began to transform the bridge into a magnificent garden. After the bridge suffered structural damage, local businesspeople and residents pitched in to fund its restoration, which was completed in 1984. Today the Bridge of Flowers continues to delight visitors from around the world.

BUY LOCAL! IT'S DELICIOUS!

When Alice Waters opened her restaurant Chez Panisse in Berkeley, California, in 1971, she was one of the first chefs to promote buying and growing food locally. "Go to the farmers' market," she'd say. "You'll get something that's delicious." Buying local also makes sense. You don't need to use lots of fuel to transport food long distances. True, not all products are available in areas with a short growing season, but greenhouse and ***hydroponic*** gardening help make a lot of produce available year-round. As for Chez Panisse, it's thriving and serving locally grown food more than 50 years after it first opened.

The Bridge of Flowers in Shelburne Falls, Massachusetts, draws locals and visitors with its colorful flowers and plants.

(LEFT) PICS721/SHUTTERSTOCK.COM; (RIGHT) PEETERV/GETTY IMAGES

> **"What you do makes a difference, and you have to decide what kind of difference you want to make."**
>
> —JANE GOODALL, PRIMATOLOGIST AND CONSERVATIONIST

A FOOD FOREST

In 2010 Ron Finley, who lives in South Los Angeles, got tired of traveling long distances to get fresh produce. He dug up a strip of land between his house and the street and started planting fruits and vegetables. City officials told him that his "food forest" was illegal. He petitioned to get the law changed—and won. Today Finley helps communities use neglected spaces around Los Angeles to create green spaces for gardens. "A garden can change people's lives," he says. "It can change the destruction of a community."

Gardeners Begin Young

Emma Biggs has gardened since she was a toddler. She published *Gardening with Emma* as a teen in 2019.

Q: What drew you to gardening?

A: I started gardening because I helped my dad in the garden when I was little. As I got older, I became a gardener in my own right and started taking over some of my dad's garden.

Q: How has your interest grown since then?

A: My interest in gardening stemmed from tomatoes. I wanted to grow as many as I could. I've kept growing tomatoes since then, but I also grow a wide range of other veggies. I've gotten into seed saving so I can help preserve all the varieties I grow. All that led me to working at an urban farm in Toronto for a couple of years.

Q: What are some ways kids can get into gardening?

A: Give kids the resources they need to explore and experiment with gardening. One important thing to remember is that gardening should be fun! An adult's idea of a garden and a kid's idea are going to be different. Let kids do what interests them, and they're more likely to become lifelong gardeners.

Walled Gardens 600 BCE

The first walled gardens were built in Persia in the sixth century BCE as places to encourage people to spend time in reflection. Later, monks in monasteries built them for quiet and prayer. Big country houses had walled gardens for growing vegetables and fruit trees. The walls kept out unwelcome visitors but also provided sheltered ***microclimates*** that protected plants and trees from wind and frost. Ireland has preserved hundreds of walled gardens such as Kylemore Abbey in County Galway. Some companies have also built modern versions of walled gardens called walled garden greenhouses. These modern structures provide a sheltered environment for plants, letting them thrive even in colder climates.

Three beautiful walled gardens, in ancient Persia, modern France and Ireland, were meant to keep intruders out and invite visitors in.

(TOP) THE NEW YORK PUBLIC LIBRARY DIGITAL COLLECTIONS/PUBLIC DOMAIN; (BOTTOM L+R) FRIEDA WISHINSKY

The St. Michael's Mount gardens are planted over sharp rocks and high walls in a hard-to-reach tidal island in Cornwall, England. Although planting was a challenge, the result is beautiful.

Planting Up, Down, Across and Over 1780

St. Michael's Mount is a tidal island in Mount's Bay, Cornwall, England. Visitors walk across to the island early in the day at low tide and return to the mainland by boat at high tide. On St. Michael's Mount there's a historic castle surrounded by beautiful terraced gardens tumbling down cliffs. The gardens were designed in 1780 for Sir John St. Aubyn, a member of parliament for the area. The gardeners who take care of the cascading plants have to repel down the rock face, roped and harnessed, to do their work. Although the jagged rocks can be dangerous, they help plants such as aloe, agave and agapanthus grow large and survive high winds and storms by absorbing heat by day and releasing it at night.

THE HIGH LINE

How did an abandoned elevated railway track in a dilapidated neighborhood in Manhattan become the High Line, a popular urban space? In 1999 two local residents, Joshua David and Robert Hammond, saw its potential and formed Friends of the High Line. Michael Bloomberg, the New York City mayor at the time, added his support, and by 2009 the first section of the High Line was built. It started as a series of 10 blocks of linked gardens running from Gansevoort Street to West 20th Street. The High Line continues to expand. It's also become a model for transforming other abandoned industrial places.

The High Line gardens in New York City attract more and more people each year. They're one of the city's top tourist attractions.
AFTON ALMARAZ/GETTY IMAGES

If you don't have a garden on the ground, try gardening on your roof!
HALFPOINT IMAGES/GETTY IMAGES

ON THE ROOF

Rooftop gardens are a great way to use available space on buildings to extend green space in a city or suburb. They also help absorb 70 percent of the rainwater during storms, which prevents streets and sewers from flooding. In 2013, in Mexico City, an unused helicopter pad on a building rooftop was transformed into a garden and co-working space called Foro Ciel. It's full of local plants and even an orchard. Irrigation is provided by rainwater and solar panels. In Rotterdam, the Netherlands, the rooftop of a building was turned into an open-air rooftop farm for growing vegetables and herbs that are sold locally. DakAkker is one of the largest rooftop farms in Europe. Local students are invited to visit and learn about growing native plants. Each student can make a "seed bomb" to toss near their school. In Vancouver, BC, the rooftop garden on the ninth floor of the Vancouver Public Library has views of downtown and the Coast Mountains. Visitors can walk among Japanese maples, arbutus trees, lavender and honeysuckle.

In 2009 Toronto became the first North American city to mandate that all new buildings with a floor area of more than 2,392 square yards (2,000 square meters) establish a green roof. Today more than 700 rooftops in the city are providing space for farming.

PARKLETS

The first ***parklet*** was built in 2005 in San Francisco. A single parking spot was converted into a temporary green space with some grass, a potted tree and a bench. Today cities like Amsterdam and Copenhagen have led the way by removing thousands of parking spaces and creating pedestrian-friendly green space instead.

FRIEDA WISHINSKY

A Green Story

Cooper Shares a Cutting

While walking down a back alley in Hermosa Beach, California, in February 2023, I came upon a cactus mini forest and a man named Cooper potting succulents beside his house. Cooper said he had missed living near a forest, so he'd created one. Then he offered me a cutting from a jade plant. I promised to nurture his gift. Sharing plant cuttings with neighbors, friends and strangers spreads the joy of green space to all of us. You can grow your own mini forest like Cooper if you have space or grow a garden on a windowsill like me.

Floating Gardens

Bangladesh is covered with wetlands that often flood. Since climate change has made floods more frequent in this Asian country, some local farmers have built floating vegetable gardens. It's a farming technique first used more than 400 years ago. Seedlings are planted in gardens made of woven weeds, which rise and fall with the changing water levels. In 2015 the Food and Agriculture Organization of the United Nations declared Bangladesh's floating gardens a globally important part of the country's agricultural heritage system.

In low-lying Bangladesh, farmers are using the old technique of growing crops on rafts made of weeds.
MOSTAFIJUR RAHMAN NASIM/SHUTTERSTOCK.COM

Saving Seeds for Our Future 2008

Plant seeds can last for a long time. The oldest recovered food seeds are 2,000 years old and were discovered near the Dead Sea, in King Herod's palace fortress of Masada in Israel. The ancient seeds have since been grown into six date palm trees that are thriving in modern Israel today. They were given biblical names—Adam, Jonah, Uriel, Boaz, Judith and Hannah.

If you have the right seeds for your local conditions, you can grow plants that feed your family and help your community.
DR. SHOSHAN HARAN

SVALBARD GLOBAL SEED VAULT

But not all seeds last that long, especially if they're exposed to moisture and heat. Since seeds are key to growing food, and the climate crisis is affecting our food supply, saving seeds has become increasingly important. Seed banks have been set up around the world. The largest, the Svalbard Global Seed Vault (also called the Doomsday Vault), houses over a million precious seeds. Opened by the Norwegian government in 2008, the vault protects the seeds of the world's food plants from global crises such as war, disease and climate change. Seeds are stored at low temperatures in a controlled environment with little moisture.

SEEDS FOR AFRICA

Drought and poverty are making growing crops difficult in Africa in the 21st century. Most farmers don't have the money to buy new seeds. They regularly used seeds from previous crops, which are often of poor quality.

Israeli scientist Shoshan Haran recognized the problem and decided to help. In 2010 she started Fair Planet, a nonprofit company dedicated to providing high-quality seeds developed specifically for the African climate and soil conditions. Her plan worked! The new seeds grew into crops 10 times better than before. To date Fair Planet has helped more than 150,000 Africans grow more and better crops on small family farms. That's helped provide food for over one million people.

Heirloom tomatoes are a little different in size, shape and color. They may not look perfect, but they taste delicious.
KLAUS VEDFELT/GETTY IMAGES

BRINGING BACK HEIRLOOM PLANTS

Since she was a kid, Desirée Shelly Flores of the Monacan Nation has loved gardening and green spaces. In 2017 she joined the Alliance of Native Seedkeepers, a network of Indigenous people who cultivate and preserve ancestral seeds. For centuries Indigenous Peoples such as the Monacan, Haudenosaunee, Sioux and Cheyenne cultivated about 300 crops in the Americas from seeds, including corn, potatoes, sunflowers, tomatoes and squash, which they then introduced to Europeans. The healthiest of these, today called ***heirloom*** or ***heritage seeds***, were saved and planted. Then they were pollinated by wind, birds, bees and other insects.

But once industrialization began, many plants were modified and grown on large farms for maximum yield, uniformity and resistance to disease. Variety and some of the great taste of heirloom plants was lost. Flores says that saving seeds is a way of keeping her history alive *and* growing delicious vegetables. She hopes to share seeds, plants and what she's learned about gardening with the next generation.

We Need Trees 1972

Trees enhance all our green spaces. They're beautiful and provide food, medicine and shelter for people and animals. They clean the air and help prevent erosion and floods. But in the 20th and 21st centuries, as we've expanded industries and housing developments, we've lost many trees.

MIYAWAKI METHOD

After years of cutting trees down, cities now realize they need trees to improve urban life. But how do you grow a tree quickly? Some cities, like Mumbai, India, have embraced the Miyawaki method, proposed in the 1980s by Japanese botanist Akira Miyawaki. By carefully preparing the soil and planting fast growing local species very densely on a small area, the trees grow quickly as they compete for sunlight. The people of Mumbai now enjoy mini forests in the heart of their bustling city.

The Tree Lady of Brooklyn

In 1964, when Hattie Carthan saw there were only three trees standing in her tough Brooklyn neighborhood of Bedford-Stuyvesant, she organized her neighbors to buy and plant trees. She soon became known as the "tree lady" of Brooklyn. A year after her death, gardens were built in an empty lot and named for Carthan. These urban gardens continue to thrive.

DAN PRATT/GETTY IMAGES

> "Indigenous communities do not clear entire forests. They cut a few trees or branches, but never entire forests... the forests and the creatures that live in it are like family to them."
>
> —CONSTANTINO AUCCA CHUTAS, CO-FOUNDER OF THE ANDEAN ECOSYSTEMS ASSOCIATION AND ONE OF THE UN'S 2022 CHAMPIONS OF THE EARTH

DEAR TREE, MELBOURNE, AUSTRALIA

Some cities have come up with innovative ways to get people to appreciate the trees in their neighborhood. In Melbourne, Australia, an interactive map was designed to help preserve the city's trees. It's called the Urban Forest Visual map, and it shows the location of more than 70,000 trees as well as their age, species and health status. It gives each tree its own email address to encourage people to help monitor its health, notifying officials of any trees needing attention. People have written letters to their favorite tree. "Dear Tree," someone wrote. "If you are that big round beautiful low hanging tree, I think you are my favorite tree. Such beauty on such an ugly road." Since the program started, about 10,000 emails have been sent to trees around Melbourne. Through these and other green-space-friendly efforts, Melbourne has become known for its leafy suburbs and urban gardens.

The people in Melbourne, Australia, know that trees make a difference in their lives. That's why they track their trees and take care of them.

(MAIN) CHARLIE ROGERS/GETTY IMAGES; (INSET) A COLLABORATION BETWEEN CITY OF MELBOURNE AND OOM CREATIVE, MELBOURNEURBANFOREST.COM.AU

WHAT CITY HAS THE MOST TREES?

As of 2023, the eight cities with the most trees are: Tampa Bay, United States; Bukit Timah, Singapore; Oslo, Norway; Vancouver, Canada; Brisbane, Australia; Montreal, Canada; Durban, South Africa; and Sacramento, United States. The World Economic Forum has pledged to grow, restore and conserve a trillion trees by 2030.

Being around trees make us feel happier and healthier.
PAMELAJOEMCFARLANE/GETTY IMAGES

1988
Bryant Park restoration
1895
Albert Kahn Museum and Gardens
BRYANT PARK
1976
Santa Monica Community Gardens
2021
Indigenous Plant and Pollinator Garden

SEVEN

GREEN SPACE BUILDS COMMUNITY

Green space doesn't just keep us healthier, provide food and shelter and prevent natural disasters. Parks and gardens bring people together. Conversations begin. People smile and relax. Kids run and play. People feel more connected and safer. A 2023 study by researchers at Cornell University and the University of Maryland confirmed that green spaces make us feel happier and safer in our communities.

Community Gardens 1976

If you don't have your own garden at home, join or start a community garden.
FRIEDA WISHINSKY

Teague Weybright is the program coordinator of the Santa Monica Community Gardens program. "The three things community gardens do are build a stronger community, reduce crime and increase property values," he says. Each plot at these community gardens is different and reflects the personality of the person who lovingly tends their small green space. Weybright says that community gardens also serve as local food sources and habitats for birds, small mammals and hundreds of insect and plant species. They provide an opportunity for the community to come together and learn from each other.

WORTH THE WAIT

Michelle Grant always wanted to garden, but as a city dweller she never had the opportunity until she discovered the Santa Monica Community Gardens program. But the lots were so popular, she had to wait seven years to finally be assigned a spot. She's now gardened for a dozen years. Grant loves having a place to grow vegetables and meet a diverse group of people. "It was a lifesaver during the COVID-19 pandemic," she says.

Leslie Neale had to wait eight years for her lot, but now she's been gardening at the Main Street Community Garden for three years and loves it. The program started in 1976, she explains. "It wasn't the first in the US but was the first in our area. It started with 60 plots, and we are now up to 78." There are rules for members. The garden has to be organic, you have to keep the weeds down, and you can't plant ***invasive species***.

Community gardens are great places to meet people and grow fresh food and lovely flowers.
(LEFT) HALFPOINT/GETTY IMAGES; (RIGHT) FRIEDA WISHINSKY

GIVING BACK TO THE COMMUNITY

The Santa Monica gardeners are also giving back to their community by supporting people experiencing ***food insecurity*** and poverty. "A couple of our gardeners started a harvest donation program," says Neale. "Every month we have community breakfasts for the public and workshops in gardening." Community gardens like these ones in southern California create food, beauty and friendships!

A park brings a community together.
SIMONKR/GETTY IMAGES

A Green Story

Free, Beautiful and Safe!

All through my childhood in New York City, parks were free and safe green spaces where I could read, play, climb rocks and dream. Those green spaces were important to me and my family. We didn't own a house with a backyard or garden. But in the 1970s, when city parks became run-down and dangerous, I avoided those places. I missed the wonderful hours I'd spent in the park in every season. I wasn't the only one. In the 1980s, people recognized how parks and green spaces enriched everyone's life in a city. Money was raised to help revitalize and renovate the parks and green spaces. I no longer live in New York City, but I wander through its parks again when I visit. I love seeing other people enjoying beautiful and safe green havens in the busy city as much as I do.

Bringing Back Green Spaces 1988

If we don't take care of our urban green spaces, they often fall into neglect. They become dirty and unsafe. That's happened many times over the years in many cities. Luckily, individuals or groups have recognized how important green spaces are to everyone in a community.

BRYANT PARK

In 1884 a small public space behind what is now the 42nd Street Library in New York City was officially named Bryant Park to honor the poet and newspaper editor William Cullen Bryant, one of the main advocates for building Central Park in New York. Sadly, by the 1970s Bryant Park was neglected, and many people avoided the area. But then, in 1988, the Bryant Park Restoration Corporation organized and financed a major park cleanup. Within a few years Bryant Park had been transformed. In 1996 it won the Urban Land Institute's Excellence Award for Public Projects. Today it's a haven for city workers and visitors, who stroll along its tree-lined paths or relax on the chairs or benches to read, chat or eat, enjoying the flowers and the calm of green space in the noisy city.

CENTRAL PARK WELCOMES YOU!

Over the years Central Park, the first public park in the United States and an oasis of green in bustling New York City, also became neglected. In the 1930s, under New York City Parks Commissioner Robert Moses, the park was cleaned up and revitalized. But when New York City suffered financial problems in the 1970s, the park once again fell into disrepair. In the 1980s a group of people created the Central Park Conservancy and started to restore the park. Today the park is again a wonderful, welcoming green space. It's the most visited urban park in the United States and one of the most popular tourist sites in the world. If you walk around the park, you can hear people speaking in many languages, enjoying the park together.

Albert Kahn

Around the World in a Garden

In 1895 Albert Kahn had a dream. He wanted to create gardens out of a 10-acre (4.2-hectare) plot of land just outside Paris. His gardens would reflect the different landscapes and cultures he'd experienced and the fascinating people he'd met while traveling the world. He hoped the gardens would draw people together to talk and learn about different cultures in a peaceful green space. The result was beautiful gardens that brought together English, French and Japanese elements. The Albert Kahn Museum and Gardens draw thousands of visitors from around the world.

FOTOFANTASTIKA/GETTY IMAGES

People come together to build Indigenous healing gardens in Canada.
JAMES FORSEY PHOTOGRAPHY

Taking Care of the Land Together 2015

Indigenous healing gardens can be found across Canada. The National Healing Forests Initiative began in 2015 when two friends, Patricia Stirbys, a member of the Cowessess First Nation in Saskatchewan, and Peter Croal, a Canadian government geologist, went on a walk in Ottawa after the final report of the ***Truth and Reconciliation Commission*** was released. They decided to start an organization that would encourage Indigenous and non-Indigenous people to create green spaces together where they could share stories, history and delight in nature. They have since partnered with groups like the David Suzuki Foundation to establish around 27 healing forests across Canada.

Connecting Rivers, Green Space and People

In 2021 UNESCO created the world's first five-country biosphere reserve, which includes Hungary, Austria, Serbia, Slovenia and Croatia. The designation will help preserve green space, rivers, wildlife and communities in those countries. It encourages community cooperation to preserve the natural resources that affect the more than 900,000 people living in those areas.

INDIGENOUS PLANT AND POLLINATOR GARDEN

In July 2021 one of these special green spaces, the Indigenous Plant and Pollinator Garden, opened at Colwood City Hall on Vancouver Island. "It's exciting to open the garden because it will ground us with our past and guide us into our future," said Sit-a-luk Raymond Peter, a Quw'utsun Nation Elder.

No matter how young or old you are, working in a garden connects you to your neighbors.
RICK STIEBEL, GOLDSTREAM NEWS GAZETTE/ BLACK PRESS MEDIA

STANDING UP FOR TREES

Many Indigenous leaders have taken on governments and powerful companies to protect their ancestral way of life, including the environment and trees in their traditional territories. When Nemonte Nenquimo, a member of the Waorani Nation of the Amazon region of Ecuador, and the 2020 UN Champion of the Earth, won a lawsuit banning the deforestation of 500,000 acres (2,023 square kilometers) of her ancestral land, she proved that political action can help save the environment and our green spaces.

Nemonte Nenquimo at a demonstration calling for climate action.
(TOP) JOHN GOMEZ/SHUTTERSTOCK.COM; (BOTTOM) JARNOVERDONK/GETTY IMAGES

SOLSTOCK/GETTY IMAGES

Designing Green Spaces for Everyone

Franklin D. Roosevelt served as president of the United States from 1933 to 1945, and he spent most of those years on crutches or in a wheelchair after contracting ***polio***. During his long presidency, Roosevelt advocated for protecting green spaces and expanding the National Park Service. Despite that, it's only in recent years that more parks have built paths that are accessible to all people.

Today the US National Park Service gives free passes to people with disabilities, and parks like Yellowstone have paths that everyone can use. Despite the advances made to create accessible green space, Alvaro Silberstein, an active outdoor adventurer who uses a wheelchair, feels that more can be done. His organization, Wheel the World, advocates for accessible tourism.

There's something special about a tree. Avid gardener Judy Illsley stands beside a giant tree near a Scottish castle.
FRIEDA WISHINSKY

My Green Story Continues

I met Judy Illsley and John Crawford in 2016 in the Yucatan in Mexico. We only spoke for a few hours, but a friendship bloomed as we shared our love of travel and gardens. That friendship grew when I visited their home and amazing garden in Scotland. Their garden has many levels and is multipurposed. It has shade and sunlight. It has a vast vegetable growing area, towering trees, shrubs and a variety of flowers.

Judy and John believe green space brings people together. Here are some words from Judy's journal that express her feelings about gardens and community:

"Tending a garden is like building and sustaining a relationship with our friends or family: being bold, nurturing, experimenting and never giving up, while also recognizing when things don't work and trying something else," she wrote. "As we encouraged flowers, shrubs and trees to flourish, we added color and life to our world, and we have created a green space that makes us happy, that changes with every season and that feels good to be in."

Judy expressed my feelings about our garden too. I created a city garden around a big silver maple tree in our backyard. Instead of grass, we had mulch and paths. The paths led to hidden spots in the garden. My garden was a magical place where I welcomed my community of friends, neighbors and family.

Today I'm living in an apartment just as I did when I was growing up. I miss my garden, but I'm grateful for south-facing windows that allow me to grow a mini garden. I'm grateful for a view of trees and green space. I'm grateful for urban parks. I'm grateful for trees and flowers on bustling city streets.

I'm grateful for green space.

Let's preserve our green spaces.

Let's create more in the future.

Let's make sure we all have green stories to share.

Green space matters to everyone.

My urban garden gave me joy. It changed with the seasons and was a haven of shade on a hot summer day. Most of all it welcomed my community of friends and family.
FRIEDA WISHINSKY

It feels good to walk through a meadow full of wildflowers.
KRIT OF STUDIO OMG/GETTY IMAGES

GLOSSARY

aqueducts—structures such as canals, pipes or tunnels that conduct water from its source to where it will be distributed

biodiversity—the variety of life on earth in all forms, from bacteria and animals to plants and trees and coral reefs

biome—a large area that has a specific climate and living things. It's often named for the dominant type of vegetation. For example, the Amazon rainforest is the largest rainforest biome.

biosphere reserve—a protected area for the conservation and protection of plants and animals, designated as such by the United Nations Educational, Scientific and Cultural Association (UNESCO)

blight—a plant disease that spoils or damages the plant

botanical garden—a collection of plants that is used for scientific study, conservation, education and display

chrysalis—the hard case that encloses a caterpillar before it changes into a butterfly

deforestation—the clearing or cutting down of trees in a forest

drought—a long period of low rainfall that often leads to a shortage of water

ecosystems—communities or groups of living things that share an environment

erosion—the gradual wearing down of a feature by wind, water or glacial ice

Fertile Crescent—a crescent-shaped area in the Middle East that extends from the Persian Gulf to the Nile River Valley. Some of the earliest civilizations lived here, such as the Egyptians, the Sumerians and the Babylonians.

food insecurity—limited or insecure access to food

fungicides—chemicals that destroy fungi, which damage plants

golden-headed langur—1 of 25 of the most critically endangered primates, a group of highly developed mammals that includes monkeys and apes. The golden-headed langurs live in the rainforests on the steep limestone cliffs of Cat Ba National Park.

heirloom/heritage seeds—seeds from plants that have been selected and grown locally for generations

hunter-gatherers—people who moved from place to place and survived by hunting, fishing and gathering food that grew in the wild

hydroponic—relating to or growing plants in sand, gravel or liquid rather than in soil

industrial farms—farms that engage in intensive, large-scale production of crops and animals, using such strategies, for example, as keeping livestock confined indoors to maximize the use of space

invasive species—organisms that are not native to an area and when introduced overwhelm and harm the native or local species

Lake District National Park—the largest national park in England. It was declared a UNESCO World Heritage site in 2017, and many writers and artists have been inspired by its beauty.

mangrove trees—tropical evergreens with large roots. Mangroves do well in wet soil and salt water.

microclimates—climates in small areas that differ from the climate around them because of wind, light and temperature

Moreton Bay fig trees—evergreens that like full sun and can live for more than 150 years

national monument—a place of scenic, historic or scientific significance that is set aside to be preserved and protected

papyrus—the material from the tall stem of a water plant, used in ancient Mediterranean cultures like Egypt for writing, painting and making ropes, sandals or boats

parklet—a small area with green space and seating, placed near sidewalks and created out of former parking spaces

pesticides—substances created to destroy insects but which are often harmful to people, animals and other plants

polio—a disabling, contagious and sometimes life-threatening disease. In 1955 a vaccine became available to prevent polio.

pollinators—agents such as insects, birds, bats and wind that transfer pollen grains from the male part of a flower (anther) to the female part (stigma). The fertilized plant can then produce seeds, fruits and young plants.

rationed—distributed equally and sparingly, allowing each person only a certain amount of a commodity or food

reservoirs—large natural or human-made lakes where water is stored

seagrasses—any of various plants with narrow, grasslike leaves that grow in the sea. Seagrasses evolved from land plants and have seeds, roots, leaves and flowers.

tenant farmers—people who farm rented land

toxic—poisonous and harmful

Truth and Reconciliation Commission of Canada—a commission designed to create a historical record of residential schools and their effects on Survivors and their families. The final report included 94 recommendations to further reconciliation with Indigenous Peoples.

UNESCO Man and Biosphere—a program that aims to achieve harmony between humans and their environment by designating special places where people can learn how to live *with* the living world rather than at its expense

UNESCO World Heritage site—a place designated as unique and special, giving it legal protection against decay and destruction. There are currently about 1,200 places around the world that are UNESCO World Heritage sites.

village common—a green space in the middle of a village where people gather or celebrate

RESOURCES

Print

Biggs, Emma, and Steven Biggs. *Gardening with Emma: Grow and Have Fun—A Kid-to-Kid Guide*. Storey Publishing, 2019.

Burnett, Frances Hodgson. *The Secret Garden*. Frederick Stokes Company, 1911.

Carson, Rachel. *Silent Spring*. Houghton Mifflin, 1962.

Goldberger, Miriam. *Taming Wildflowers: Bringing the Beauty and Splendor of Nature's Blooms Into Your Own Backyard*. St. Lynn's Press, 2014.

Paulsen, Gary. *Hatchet*. Atheneum, 2000.

Seuss, Dr. *The Lorax*. Random House, 1971.

Stewart-Sharpe, Leisa. *The Green Planet*. BBC Children's Books, 2022.

Upjohn, Rebecca. *The Last Loon*. Orca Book Publishers, 2010.

Wishinsky, Frieda. *A Flower Is a Friend*. Pajama Press, 2023.

Wishinsky, Frieda. *The Man Who Made Parks: The Story of Parkbuilder Frederick Law Olmsted*. Tundra Books, 2009.

Wohlleben, Peter. *Can You Hear the Trees Talking? Discovering the Hidden Life of the Forest*. Greystone Kids, 2019.

Online

BBC Earth: bbcearth.com

BBC History for Kids: bbc.co.uk/history/forkids/index.shtml

Britannica Kids: kids.britannica.com

CBC Kids: cbc.ca/kids/

Discover the Forest: discovertheforest.org

History for Kids: historyforkids.net

National Geographic Kids: kids.nationalgeographic.com

National Wildlife Federation: nwf.org

Time for Kids: timeforkids.com

World Wildlife Fund: worldwildlife.org

Young People's Trust for the Environment: ypte.org.uk

ACKNOWLEDGMENTS

The expression "It takes a village" is especially true for writing books.

Many wonderful people helped make *Keep Our World Green* grow and bloom, starting with my insightful and supportive editor Kirstie Hudson. This is our fourth book together, and even though each one has focused on a big topic, Kirstie has made the revision process a pleasure. Thanks also to copyeditor Vivian Sinclair. Copyediting is an art. I appreciate the creativity of designer Dahlia Yuen and artist Sara Theuerkauf to enhance the look, flow and feel of a book that touches on the importance of beautiful places. And thanks so much to publishers Ruth Linka and Andrew Wooldridge. I am a fan of all your fine, kid-friendly and thoughtful books and feel honored to call myself an Orca writer.

Many thanks to my husband Bill Wishinsky for his support, wise comments and for happily joining me on many green space adventures around the world.

Many friends have contributed to this book by generously sharing stories and photos of how green space has impacted their lives. My heartfelt thanks to Amy and Lauren Irwin, Beverly Katz Rosenbaum, Rebecca Upjohn, Jennifer Baum, Tom Miller, Miriam Koral, Genevieve Jost, Miriam Goldberger, Elisabeth Neumann, Iwona Ziembinska, Linda Rosenbaum, Reggie Morgan, Harriet Zaidman, Mollie Sugimoto, Emma Biggs, Steve Biggs, John Crawford and Judy Illsley.

My deepest appreciation to Shoshan Haran, Teague Weybright, Michelle Grant, Leslie Neale, Bernard Dichek, Mark O'Callaghan, Natalie Maclagan and Sarah Cedar Miller for sharing their experiences, knowledge and journey with green spaces.

INDEX

*Page numbers in **bold** indicate an image caption.*

From the PAST to the PRESENT and into the FUTURE!

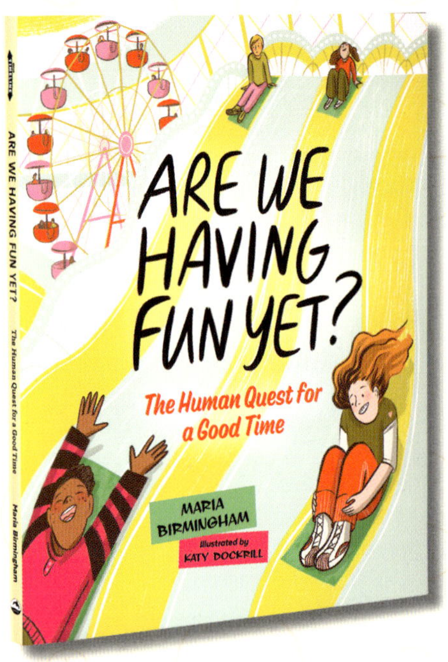

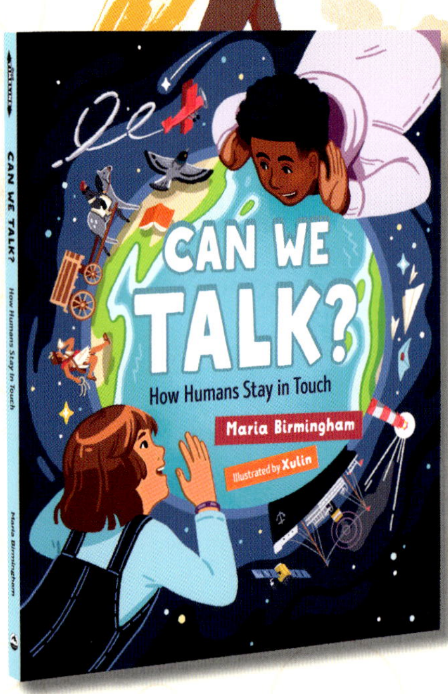

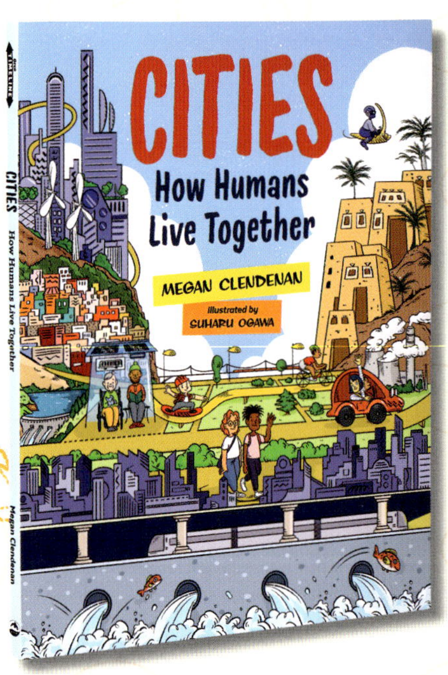

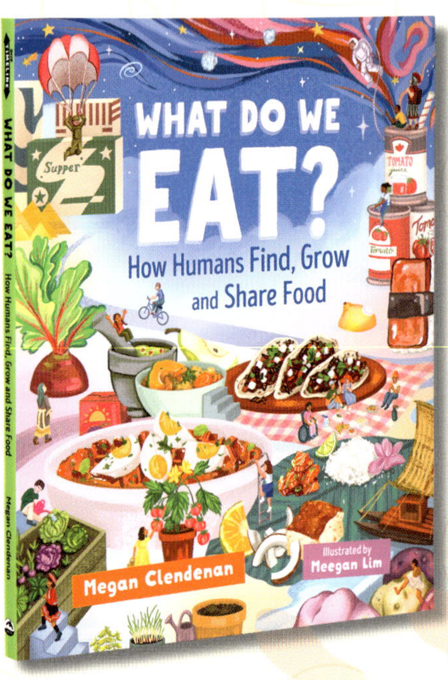

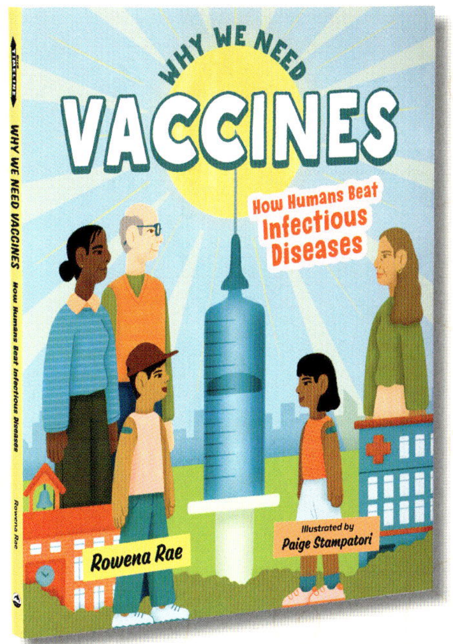

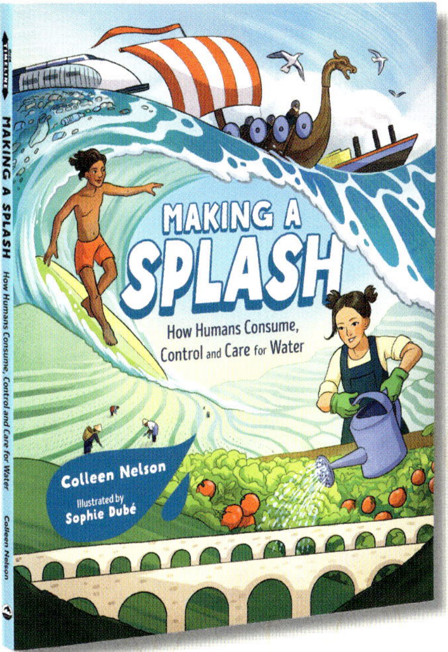

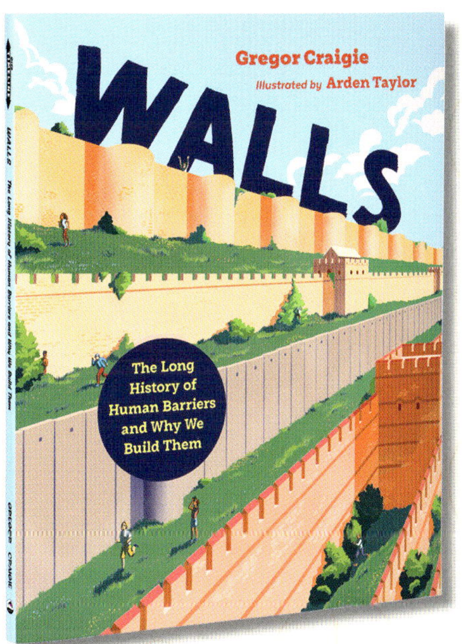

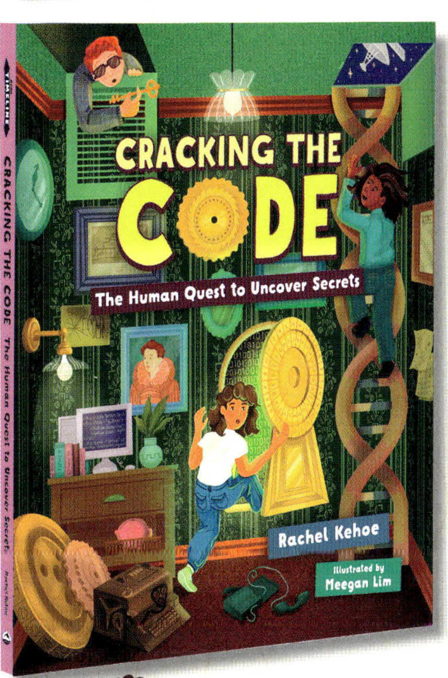

The Orca Timeline series explores how big ideas have shaped humanity. Discover what our collective history can tell us about the planet today and tomorrow.

Bill Wishinsky

Frieda Wishinsky is the international award-winning author of over 80 picture books, novels and nonfiction. Her books have been translated into many languages, including Spanish, Hungarian, Polish, Russian, French, Chinese and Korean. Frieda loves exploring new ideas and sharing the writing process with writers and readers of all ages. Frieda also loves to travel and take pictures. She enjoys walks and talks with friends and family, eating chocolate and, of course, visiting parks, gardens and green spaces everywhere.

Anthony Roach

Sara Theuerkauf is an illustrator and interior architect. Her work captures moments of simple ritual coziness and reflects her affinity for nature, textiles, traditional craft, maps and design. Her best ideas for sketches come to her on long walks through the forest or botanical gardens near her studio in Vancouver.